FROM ABERYSTWYTH
TO SAN FRANCISCO

By the same author:

Translation of:

Travels of a Welsh Preacher in the USA: Peregrinations of William Davies Evans during the later nineteenth century

From Aberystwyth
to San Francisco:
the Welsh Community in America
in the late nineteenth century

Margaret Morgan Jones

First published in 2013

© Margaret Morgan Jones

© Gwasg Carreg Gwalch 2013

Published with the financial support
of the Welsh Books Council

ISBN: 978-1-84527-457-3

Cover design: Eleri Owen

Published by Gwasg Carreg Gwalch,
12 Iard yr Orsaf, Llanrwst, Wales LL26 0EH
tel: 01492 642031
fax: 01492 641502
email: books@carreg-gwalch.com
website: www.carreg-gwalch.com

Contents

List of Welsh-language newspapers mentioned in the text

Name	Translation	Dates
Baner ac Amserau Cymru	The Banner and Times of Wales	1857–1910
Bedydd Clasurol	Classical Baptism	1877
Y Cenhadwr (Americanaidd)	The American Missionary	1840–1904
Y Cyfaill (o'r Hen Wlad yn America)	The Friend from the Old Country in America	1838–1933
Y Drych	The Mirror	1856–present
Y Drysorfa	The Treasurehouse	1831–1968
Y Glorian	The Scales	1872–1894
Y Methodist	The Methodist	1852–56
Seren Orllewinol	Western Star	1844–1866
Y Wasg	The Press	1871–1890
Y Wawr (Americanaidd)	The American Dawn	1872–1896

Foreword
Dr David Lloyd, Syracuse

When my parents emigrated from Wales (via Liverpool) in 1948 to join the Welsh-American community in Utica, New York, they settled into a prosperous manufacturing city. Utica's immigrant populations were large and various – mainly Polish, Italian, Irish, and Welsh. My father answered a call to serve as minister for Welsh parishioners of Moriah Presbyterian Church (built in 1883), where he preached in Welsh and English during the early years of his ministry. Over the course of the twentieth century, the Welsh community of Utica expanded and flourished, then assimilated and dispersed, as immigration from Wales slowed then halted altogether. My mother, who died in 2011, age ninety-seven, was the last native Welsh-speaker in the region. In 2007 Moriah – the single surviving Welsh church in Utica – was sold to Seventh Day Adventists.

Who will remember the Welsh who built Moriah – the families who worshipped, sang hymns, gossiped in Welsh on the sidewalk outside the front doors following each service for over a hundred years? Farmers, carpenters, secretaries, milkmen, mothers, fathers, businessmen, railway workers. Who will document how they lived – and their concerns, fears, aspirations?

I'm happy to report that there's been an intensifying interest in uncovering and documenting the Welsh experience in the United States in recent years, including academic studies, documentaries, and collections of personal letters. One of the earliest authors to publish contemporaneous reports on the lives of Welsh Americans was Rev. William Davies Evans, in articles written for *Baner ac Amserau Cymru*. Selections of these are translated and collected by Evans' great-niece Margaret Morgan Jones in *From Aberystwyth to San Francisco: the Welsh Community in America in the Late Nineteenth Century.* These writings are dispatches from the immigrant frontiers of the United States, describing Welsh settlements from Manhattan to San Francisco, with excursions into fascinating nooks and crannies as Rev. Evans made his way across the country, mostly by train. He recorded what he saw and heard 'as news because these events will go down in history' (his own words). In doing so, he animates for his readers the varied, exciting, often hardscrabble world of Welsh immigrant experience.

Rev. Evans projects a distinctive voice and firmly-held opinions. He's a booster of Welsh emigration. He's religious, regularly taking the pulse of chapels he visits. He believes that temperance can solve the world's ills. He honors habits of frugality and hard work. He's proud of being Welsh, paying careful attention to where the language is thriving in the 'new world' and where declining. But he has one particular quality that makes *From Aberystwyth to San Francisco* such a pleasure. He's *curious*. What is the best way to arrange travel from Aberystwyth to New York? Should one book in the saloon or steerage? Rev. Evans provides the answers. How much does an acre of land cost in Bala, Kansas? ($20.) How much would a quarryman in Granville, Ohio earn for a day's labour? (A dollar and a half.)

In *From Aberystwyth to San Francisco* the reader can accompany Rev. Evans on a fascinating journey. You'll learn that the Welsh in Slatington, Pennsylvania, were fluent in three languages: Welsh, English, and German. You'll experience a 'Negro Revival' service. You'll meet the sinful 'German freethinkers' of New Ulm, Minnesota. In late 1880, when Rev. Evans arrived in Manhattan, the United States was still recovering from the devastating Civil War of

1861–65. The gunfight at the OK Corral in Tombstone, Arizona, would take place in 1881, the same year President Garfield was assassinated (an event Rev. Evans mentions). But this author rarely dwells on public traumas. His main concern is with the daily lives of Welsh immigrants – and with recording details, characters, and interactions that lesser writers might overlook, as in this passage about Native American women in St Paul, Minnesota:

> They had brought animal skins to the market to be sold or exchanged for white man's merchandise. I was tempted to speak to these ladies and I approached one that was crouching, since she appeared more Indian than the others. I asked her: 'Where do you live?' I must have frightened her because she picked herself up and ran to a nearby building with her face to the wall, similar to a small child who thinks that he is out of sight if he looks the other way. After not succeeding with that one, I turned to another two who were leaning on a ladder and I asked them the same question. They soon realised that I meant no harm because they smiled but did not say anything. 'No English?' I continued. They shook their heads and smiled again. As I walked away, I noticed that these two were having fits of laughter at the expense of the frightened one. They laughed and laughed until they were shaking and since one of them was quite plump, she caused quite a tremor – to put it mildly! The one that had been afraid realised that she had not been in danger after all, and soon returned to join the others with a peevish look on her face.

Here Rev. Evans reports an unusual convergence: a Welsh minister visiting a Midwestern city using his second language to communicate with native women who speak their own language. 'Where do you live?' he asks, because he's curious – where do people live whose land has been seized, who find their way to a city center to buy 'white man's merchandise' without speaking the white man's language? He sees these women, registers their fear, recognises their humanity. It's a vignette about danger and safety, with telling details: after all, the merchandise the women seek is precisely what will destroy their way of life. And 'way of life' is at the forefront of Rev. Evans' articles, whether it be the survival techniques of recent immigrants; or the ways of life of the Welsh back home, now blurring and mutating in the crucible of the new world.

In chapter 4 of *From Aberystwyth to San Francisco*, Rev. Evans describes his visit to Utica, 'the Athens of the United States' as he terms it, in 1880. He finds that the city's 'chapel-buildings have galleries and are very grand'. Had Rev. Evans visited in 1883, when Moriah Church – my family's church – had been newly built to accommodate Welsh immigrants to the region, I'm sure he would have noted the solid and spacious structure, the Welsh words carved into stone and wood, the gallery overlooking pews packed with parishioners. He would have asked questions of those chatting on the sidewalk after the service. He would have listened to their stories. And he'd write about what he'd seen and heard.

David Lloyd
Le Moyne College
Syracuse, New York
USA
Summer 2013

Introduction

This book, *From Aberystwyth to San Francisco*, is a continuation of the translation of Reverend W. D. Evans' book *Dros Gyfanfor a Chyfandir* [Over Ocean and Continent], published by the *Cambrian News*, Aberystwyth, in 1883. *Dros Gyfanfor a Chyfandir* was translated from Welsh into English by me, William Davies Evans' great-niece, and published as *Travels of a Welsh Preacher in the USA* (Gwasg Carreg Gwalch, March 2008).

Throughout that book, Evans mentions another, entitled *Hanes Taleithiau America A'r Cymry Ynddynt* [The History of the United States of America and the Welsh Living in Them], which he was preparing for publication. Why this book never saw the light of day remained a mystery – until I discovered an explanation in an article written by Mr H. Richards of Otter, Iowa, and published in *Y Drych*, 9 April 1896. Mr Richards portrays Mr Evans' story and discusses the fate of the manuscript thus:

From the southern slopes of Trichrug, Cardiganshire, one can catch sight of one of the most scenic glades in the world. The river Aeron meanders through a valley which gradually widens as the river flows towards the sea and there are large trees rising in the shape of an Amphitheatre along the way. Forming the countryside are the village of Talsarn, St Hilary's Church, Abermeurig Chapel, the mansions of Abermeurig, Llanllyr and Gelli, as well as sightings of various lime-washed farmhouses and hedged-in-fields. This scene creates a very paradisean picture. On a smallholding, by the name of Wern Fach, in this valley, on 23rd February 1842, Reverend William Davies Evans was born. He was

a descendant of a priestly lineage, namely, Reverend
Lewis Evans, Llanfihangel-geneu'r Glyn and his son,
Reverend Lewis Evans, MA – headmaster of Edward
Richard School, Ystrad Meurig. He was also related to
Mr D. Davies, MP, Llandinam and Mr Lewis Pugh, MP,
Abermad.

He came to this country with his parents when he
was young and joined the Calvinistic Methodists in
Newark, Ohio. Before long, his articles began appearing
in *Y Cyfaill*. Dr Rowlands, the editor of this paper,
showed a marked enthusiasm for Evans' contributions.
In 1867, he was encouraged by church members in
Columbus, Ohio, to preach the Gospel. After spending
time studying at the Institutes of Delaware and Oberlin
and acting as pastor in churches at Youngstown,
Weathersfield and Church Hill, he sailed to Wales in
1872 with the intention of a short stay, but his diaries
kept filling up with so many requests to conduct religious
services that he made his home in his motherland for
fifteen years. During this period, in 1876, he married Jane
Jones, Penwernhir, Pontrhydfendigaid.

Leaving his family in Wales, Reverend Evans sailed
to America towards the end of 1880; sponsored by
railroad companies, he visited almost every Welsh
institution from the Atlantic to the Pacific. Whilst doing
so, he wrote a detailed account of his experiences – both
materialistic and spiritual. He wrote hundreds of letters
and collected books and papers relating to Welsh people.
His main aim was to publish a book entitled *Hanes
Taleithiau Unedig America a'r Cymry Ynddynt*. He visited
the main agricultural lands of the West and had a taste of
the amazing wonders of this country. His articles were
published weekly in *Baner ac Amserau Cymru*. On his
return to Wales in the spring of 1882, he was incited by

many to compile an account of his travels in book format. This he did, in spite of his apprehensions. *Dros Gyfanfor a Chyfandir* has been evaluated by some eminent critics of our nation as one of the most interesting books in the Welsh language.

Although this book is an excellent publication, in monetary value it has been a loss. Its sales proved to be disappointing, mainly because much of its content had been serialised beforehand in *Baner Ac Amserau Cymru*. This predicament made him decide not to print *Hanes Taleithiau Unedig America a'r Cymry Ynddynt*. It is a great pity that he was not given enough support to publish this second book as I am sure it would have been of significant interest to us as a nation. Early in 1887 he returned to this country again – with his family this time, with the aim of selling copies of *Dros Gyfanfor a Chyfandir*. However, the following year, he came up with the idea of embarking on a weekly newspaper. He was sponsored by friends in Long Creek, Iowa, and Emporia, Kansas, and spent almost a year travelling, at his own expense, to try and persuade people to subscribe to this venture before the launch of Columbia on July 4th 1888. He was editor of this paper for three years and, according to him, under difficult circumstances. He experienced opposition by people who would have benefitted in the long run, if only they had supported him. To dwell on his commitment to be of service to his compatriots and the way he was treated, would fill many copies of *Y Drych*. All will be revealed on the last day.

Afterwards, he decided to move to Kansas City where he became like John in the desert (Luke 1:80) – out of circulation. Fortunately, by now, he has regained his passion for preaching with more enthusiasm than ever. Not only is Mr Evans a skilful writer but he is also a good and invaluable preacher. He is not gifted with a very melodious voice, nor is he as eloquent as some preachers in his presentation, but the substance of his sermons is as commendable as that of any preacher and he delivers his message with such vigour and passion that it is glued in the minds of his congregation. Occasionally, no doubt, he is ahead of his time regarding an insight into some topics. He has steadfast ideals and a vivid imagination and is able to deliver his sermons in a charming and appealing manner. He explains his text allegorically and his delivery is practical and philosophical. According to the plan of the GREAT MASTER, his sermons seem to aim at making his congregation understand the grounding of his text rather than embracing feelings. May this good man have many more years to promote good tidings.

H. Richards, Otter, Iowa – Y Drych, *April 9, 1896*

This article by Mr Richards has thrown light on the fact that *Hanes Taleithiau America a'r Cymry Ynddynt* was never published. My great-uncle had become depressed and had decided not to continue with his initial dream.

To my delight, I discovered forty of my great-uncle's 'Letters' in nineteenth-century editions of *Baner ac Amserau Cymru* at the National Library of Wales, Aberystwyth. These letters are entitled *O Aberystwyth i San Francisco* [From Aberystwyth to San Francisco] and each one is numbered. On the basis of these findings, I have selected, translated and compiled passages which I am sure would have been included in the book *Hanes Taleithiau Unedig America a'r Cymry Ynddynt*, had it been released. Apart from occasional references, I have refrained from repeating any text that was included in *Travels of a Welsh Preacher in the*

USA. I have concentrated on what my great-uncle wrote about the circumstances and day-to-day life of Welsh settlers in America. Reverend Evans was born in Wern Fach, but was closely related to the Berth Neuadd household in the neighbourhood of Talsarn. San Francisco was named after St Francis of Assisi, but is renowned today for its Golden Gate Bridge, opened in 1937.

The system of translation I have adopted involved certain sensitivities relating to nationality, race and religion. Many mid-nineteenth century terms have greatly changed in meaning and this raises issues of what has now become known as 'political correctness'. This applies particularly to certain racial descriptions. I have, generally speaking, retained the mid nineteenth-century forms, urging the reader to remember that these may not have had the same connotations as they now have and certainly William Davies Evans did not inflict any discrimination against any of the people of various ethnicities with whom he came into contact. Place-names, in some cases, have undergone spelling changes, while others no longer exist. The reader should be able to follow Reverend W. D. Evans' route by rail, horse and foot with the aid of any map of the United States of America.

Although the Golden Gate Bridge opened in 1937, it has become one of the major landmarks in San Francisco, and therefore it has been included on the cover of this book, together with the original building of Aberystwyth University.

Margaret Morgan Jones
Lampeter, 2013

1

How to Travel to America

After taking pictures of my childhood haunts in Cardiganshire with my camera, in order to show them to my brothers and friends in America and after inviting several neighbours to a prayer meeting in our home at Pontrhydfendigaid, with the purpose of asking God for his blessing on my travels and also His protection over my family during my absence, I started my journey on 19th November, 1880. Although it was a wrench to say goodbye to my wife, Jane, and my young sons, I did not want to show too much emotion so as not to appear childish.

I boarded the train for Liverpool in Aberystwyth and when I reached my destination, Mr J. D. Pierce, an emigration agent, took charge of me. Mr Pierce was recommended to me by ministers of various denominations and this is the main reason I have put my trust in him. At this point I would like to advise prospective emigrants of the available avenues they can pursue in order to ensure safety for themselves, their families and their possessions.

There are two choices when purchasing a regular ticket; one option covers only the voyage whilst the other incorporates the crossing plus the conveyance to a town near to the intended destination in America. However, if you purchase either of these tickets, no one is at hand to care for you when you reach Liverpool. You have to look after yourselves, and if you are not familiar with this city, finding suitable accommodation is sometimes a problem, especially if there are young children and luggage to care for. A better choice is to engage a reputable agent in Liverpool to reserve a place for you on a ship. This agent would then meet you on your arrival in Liverpool to ensure that transport is at hand for conveyance to comfortable lodgings and afterwards to the ship. This service is free because agents are paid by the companies which engage them. If the agent is a person of integrity, he makes sure that you are not overcharged for accommodation and transportation of your luggage. Be on the lookout for sharpers though – persons who are more concerned with their own interests than your well-being. I do know of some people who have paid the price for engaging such agents.

It is appropriate that I advise you regarding the class systems obtainable on transatlantic ships, since the differences are quite substantial. There is a choice between saloon and steerage, making one imagine that the shipping companies were only accommodating wealthy, influential people on the one hand or illiterate, poor people on the other. This is not entirely true, since some ships also have provision for people who are considered middle-class. Such people are called the Intermediate Passengers. I believe that only the Guion Line[1] provides saloon class for people sailing from Liverpool to New York; the Allan Line[2] ships people from Liverpool to Boston and the American Line[3] provides a service from Liverpool to Philadelphia. Each one of these Lines grants open railroad tickets to Boston, New York and Philadelphia, so long as one sails with them to their destined harbour. The price of a saloon ticket can be 18, 15 or 12 guineas, depending how far the sleeping quarters are from the engines. The nearer one is to the centre of the ship, the louder the noise and more vibration is experienced than in other areas. This is the reason why cabins in this section are cheaper. On the other hand, the nearer one is to the rudder or helm, or the front part, the more one feels the movement of the ship as it sways on the waves. As far as I am concerned, I prefer the noise of the engines to the oscillation of the ship and I had no hesitation in opting for the cheaper berth.

Catering is first class in the saloon and the passengers have access to all amenities available in this quarter, which has furnishings such as easy-chairs, floor coverings, a library, piano and suchlike. If you can afford the saloon, all the better, and if you can avoid sea-sickness, you should have a very enjoyable voyage; but if you suffer from this complaint you could be very uncomfortable and it will not matter to you whether you are in the saloon or another area. No doubt, most passengers from Wales will not be saloon travellers.

Furthermore, I wish to make you aware of the considerable differences between the intermediate and steerage sectors. The price of intermediate is eight guineas and included in the charge is a berth which consists of a comfortable bed and nice, clean bed-linen. One small cabin is shared by four and it has a daily room service. The following amenities are provided: a washstand, crockery, towels, mirror and a rug as floor covering. If you are unwell, meals are served in the cabins. Meals for intermediate passengers are laid on a long table in a designated room. There are three nourishing, well-prepared meals provided daily – as good as you would have at home, that is, if you are careful at taking care of yourselves thus. A bill of fare, which shows what is on the menu for each day of the week, is provided with your ticket.

On the *Abyssinia*, the ship I sailed on, the concern for our well-being was better than described on the bill of fare. The price of a voyage in the steerage is six guineas but it is up to you to arrange that you have a bed or mattress, a thick blanket, tin crockery and some cutlery which can be purchased on the deck. You should also consider taking medicines with you in case of illnesses. Should you be unwell, a good tip to the steward usually guarantees a very tasty meal! That is the report I have received anyway.

Abyssinia

In view of these additional expenses, it is just as well for people who intend travelling steerage to change to intermediate. The cost, after adding up all the extras that have to be paid for in steerage, is about the same as intermediate, but without the trimmings. In steerage you have to mix with people from other countries – Irish and Germans usually. You also have to receive food in your hands, wherever you may be – without table or chairs or any kind of system. All things considered, I strongly advise you to opt for the intermediate. Apparently, the Guion Line offers the best intermediate accommodation but if you do choose steerage, the White Star Shipping Company is supposed to be good.

Maybe this narrative will not prove to be very interesting to some readers but I do wish to be of practical assistance to all emigrants, if possible.

---

[1] By 1870 the Guion Line was ranked third in the delivery of immigrants to New York.

[2] The Allan Line, founded in 1852, was instrumental in transportation of emigrants on transatlantic voyages.

[3] The American Line was formed as The American Steamship Company in 1872. The Liverpool service was discontinued in 1884.

2

The Journey; in New York

Around mid-day, on Saturday, 20th November 1880, I set foot aboard the *Abyssinia*, a vessel which the Guion company had recently purchased from Cunard. It was to be its first voyage under its new ownership, with Captain Douglas at the helm. The passengers consisted of eighteen Welsh people – six of them were either Welsh Americans (who had been born in America) or Welsh immigrants who had adopted America as their country. Mr J. H. Bevan, the purser on the *Abyssinia*, is Welsh. He is a very amiable young man who was born in Pembrokeshire and is very proud of his nationality. He told me that he admired the Calvinistic Methodists because his parents belonged to the denomination. My wish for him is that he also will get acquainted with his parents' faith. The purser is of a higher rank than the captain and all commercial responsibilities relating to the ship rest on his shoulders. I understand that many high-ranking officials pertaining to the Guion Line are Welsh, and since this company values our nation, we, the Welsh, should reciprocate.

We sailed over very choppy waters for most of the fourteen-day voyage, but all was calm by the time we reached Long Island. Years ago, the smooth-spoken sharpers of New York would meet immigrants off the ships and mislead them into buying tickets which, supposedly, would enable them to go on their way into the city. These tickets were not worth the paper they were printed on. Nowadays, government officials keep a keen eye on this misdemeanour. The most impudent people, at present, are the hackneymen and cabmen. As soon as you have passed through the custom-house, they pounce with an authoritative approach and ask the whereabouts of your destination in the city. They imply that they know the area, and if you fall into their trap they shove you and your belongings, in an off-hand way, into a large carriage and greatly overcharge you for a journey, maybe of only half a mile, whereas you could very often reach your destination on a street-car for five cents. I advise you to treat these opportunists with the same contempt that they show you. Also, mind that you go to the licensed places in Liverpool and New York to exchange money.

After I disembarked from the *Abyssinia,* I went to the temperance-house of the late John W. Jones, 53 Beach Street (a brother of *Dafydd Morganwg*).[1] Mr Jones' widow and children run the business now. This boarding-house is situated at a very convenient spot for immigrants and is very commendable. After my short stay in this house, I went to seek Reverend G. H. Humphreys. After discovering his address, finding the street was no problem, although it was quite a long journey. New York is the fourth largest city in the world.

The street-cars are almost the same as those in Britain apart from the fact that the owners have different methods of securing that no money goes into the pockets of employees. On one route, the passengers have to drop the fare (five cents) into a box which is placed at the front of the car. The one cent coin is so like the five cent one that only the passengers and the Almighty know how much is actually paid. If change is needed, say from half-a-dollar, passengers will give this coin to the driver to be exchanged for a sealed envelope containing small change of equal value. This method ensures that everybody has the correct amount of cash. Every evening, the driver has to account to his employers for all transactions. There are conductors on several routes but every system safeguards the employers from any form of cheating.

What impresses newcomers to New York first of all is the city's railroad network. It has been constructed above ground, whereas the one in London is underground. The sight of high speed trains up above is quite alarming at first glance. What if there was a derailment? However, New Yorkers are not perturbed; so far there has not been a major accident.

I stayed on the Saturday night in Robert Lewis' house. Mr Lewis is a native of Tywyn, Merionethshire, and is a very successful businessman and one of the wealthiest Welshmen in New York. He is a deacon with the Calvinistic Methodists and is very faithful to his Saviour. One can say that he is a person who has learnt the invaluable lesson that only a few can appreciate: 'The hand of the diligent maketh rich' (Proverbs 10:4). Mr Lewis' wife is the daughter of the late Reverend Thomas Jenkins, Utica. I don't suppose that either of them will read these lines, therefore I shall escape from being reprimanded for mentioning them!

The following Sunday, I went to Brooklyn, to listen to Reverend H. W. Beecher[2] in his Plymouth Church – a building of almost the same size as that of Finney's[3] in Oberlin. Some older people will remember the dynamic religious revival which was initiated by Charles G. Finney in 1840. This revival, which lasted several years, spread across a vast area of America, Great Britain and other countries. Its impact was as powerful in Wales as other parts of the globe. Reverend Lyman Beecher[4] claims that this reawakening was the most effective one since the time of the Apostles and that Finney, by means of his sermons and his book on the revival, had been a salvation of souls to hundreds of thousands of people. His book has been translated into

Plymouth Congregational Church

Reverend Henry W. Beecher

many languages, including Welsh. I had the privilege of being in this great man's congregation during the years 1870 and 1871. He was tall, serious and distinguished and although I was amongst thousands listening to him, I felt that he was talking to me personally. He could hold my concentration throughout the entire service. A reporter from Cardiff's *Evening Express* writes thus in *Y Drych*, April 9, 1905:

> The amazing similarity between the present revival in Wales and the one Charles G. Finney generated, has crossed my mind more than once during these weeks. Reading about events in newspapers makes me feel as if I was reading Finney's autobiography – stories of spiritual wonderments captivating my attention and emotion, more than any romantic story I have ever read. The resemblance is noticeable by more than one coincidence; the way both movements began and their development through the force of the Holy Spirit are so alike. On several occasions, Evan Roberts,[5] the Welsh revivalist, revealed his displeasure at the ineffective, customary prayers that were delivered in churches.

During the afternoon of this Sunday, whilst I was still in New York, I had the privilege of officiating in the Calvinistic Methodist Chapel. At one time, there were four Welsh churches in New York, each one representing a different denomination. Now, though, the Wesleyans and Baptists have stopped conducting their services in Welsh. The Congregationalists are also wavering towards the English language. The minister of the Congregational Church is Reverend D. Davies. The Calvinistic Methodists are holding their ground in the preservation of the Welsh language, with 250 members regularly taking Holy Communion; the services are well attended in a very attractive chapel in 13th Street. The minister of this Methodist church is Reverend G. H. Humphreys, a talented and versatile young man who is held in high esteem by people from all walks of life. Mr Humphreys shepherds his flock very conscientiously and conducts services in an interesting way. It is quite an accomplishment to be able to preach equally well in both English and Welsh. He is also fluent in other languages and, at one time, he would conduct his Sunday services in three languages – Welsh in the morning, English in the afternoon and German in the evening.

Many Welsh people live in New York and the surrounding area; a number of them are respected business people who are gradually integrating into the American way of life. On Monday, 6th December, I left the city, regrettably without much sightseeing. I had departed from Liverpool later than I had hoped, and because of the stormy sea-voyage I had experienced, I had been further delayed. Therefore, it was high time I started keeping my appointments; some had already been cancelled. I travelled north alongside the Hudson River which was flowing leisurely towards the sea, similar to the Dyfi by Ynys Las in Wales. The landscape was similar to the rural scenes in Wales.

---

[1] *Dafydd Morganwg* was the bardic name of David Watkin Jones (1832–1905), poet, historian and geologist, who was born in Merthyr Tudful, south Wales.

[2] Henry Ward Beecher (1813–1887): prominent Congregationalist clergyman, social reformer, American temperance co-founder and leader, born in Lichfield, Connecticut.

[3] Charles Grandison Finney (1792–1875), often called America's foremost revivalist. His lectures were reprinted in England and translated into French, Welsh and German.

[4] Lyman Beecher (1775–1863), Presbyterian Minister, father of Henry Ward Beecher.

[5] Evan John Roberts (1878–1951), Welsh Revivalist. Born in Loughor, Glamorganshire.

3

Middle Granville; Slate-quarrying; Oneida County

Around eight o'clock I arrived in the village of Middle Granville and was escorted to the cosy lodgings of Mrs Morris, a sister of Reverend Griffith Williams, Talsarnau, North Wales. Middle Granville is central to the slate quarries of this region and therefore of relevance to the entire neighbourhood. People from the Bethesda and Ffestiniog regions are the majority of Welsh people residing here; as a Welsh settlement, it goes back thirty years. The Methodists and the Congregationalists have very decorative chapels in this town. The Congregationalists do not have a minister at present, but Reverend Pugh, who lives in the locality, is very supportive. Reverend Hugh Davies is the Methodist minister; he is also bishop of Vermont and superintendent of the Calvinistic Methodists' Connection[1] in this area. By all accounts, he is fulfilling his positions very well. He was born in Bala, north Wales, but came to this country when he was very young. His first ministry was in Wisconsin but he has been in this region for some time now and the people of Vermont are so appreciative of him. Although Mr Davies is no longer young, he is still classified as one of the leading ministers within the Methodist Connection in this part of America. It was in this region that Mr Eleazer Jones, formerly of Liverpool, spent the last years of his life. He had been elected to the State Legislature for this district and was involved in movements in other areas as well. Mr Jones is greatly missed by all communities. His brother, William

Jones, still lives here and is deacon and a responsible superintendent regarding Methodist activities.

There are around thirty quarries in the neighbourhood of Middle Granville, but not every one is operating at present. Different techniques to those used in Wales are in force when slates are processed here. Green, red, purple, grey and variegated slates are the ones produced, and they vary in prices from two to six dollars per square. Different to the method practised in Wales, where slates are stacked on their sides, the custom here is to lay them flat and instead of splitting the rock on its forehead, so to speak, holes are drilled at random into the ground and the slates are then lifted through these openings.

The Welsh quarrymen would also find the practice of lifting the derricks by steam-power very strange. From the steam-engine's powerhouse, there are wire ropes leading out in all directions to the different holes; some of them hundreds of yards above the quarrying area. They can be compared to a large-scale spider's web and it is by means of these ropes, the steam-power hoists the derricks from the holes. I understand that these industries are owned by Williams, Guion and Company, and most of the managers and quarrymen are from Wales. The area does not seem to be very prosperous at the moment. On average, a quarryman earns a dollar and a half per day. However, work for women is in demand in the area and waitresses can easily find work with earnings of around seven dollars per month.

There are in this region between ten and twenty communities where Welsh people reside and there are religious Causes by Methodists and Congregationalists. Griffith and Nathaniel, two Welsh quarry owners from Ffestiniog, north Wales, live in the pretty village of Poultney. Sea-green slates are quarried in this region and most of them are dispatched to England, Russia and other countries of the Old World. From Poultney, Griffith transported me on his fast sledge to Fair Haven where many Welsh people live. Messrs Pugh and Owens, from Ffestiniog, north Wales, are owners of businesses as well as some property here. Mr Owen Owens, the respected deacon, founded the Methodist Cause in these regions around thirty years ago, and it was from Fair Haven that the good tidings spread to other areas. Mr Owens is now elderly and has suffered ill-health but is still young at heart. There are two churches in Fair Haven – Congregational and Methodist. At present, there is no Welsh minister in charge of either church, but Reverend E. D. Humphreys lives locally and although he refused to be inducted, he supports worthy activities and everyone has a good word for him.

Mr Humphreys moves around in different circles and is Town Clerk of Fair Haven which has a population of around 3,000. Apart from the drugstore, there are no pubs or shops selling alcoholic drinks here. No wonder the residents are good people. The majority of the world's inhabitants would be good, if it was not for the taverns. Fair Haven is the main town to the north of the settlement and Middle Granville, the main urban district towards the south.

On my way from New York to the quarries of Vermont, I had to travel through the following main cities: Poughkeepsie, Hudson, Albany and Troy – all situated along the Hudson River. Thence, westward to Oneida County (via Saratoga – noted for its springs), Ballston and Schenectady. After arriving in Utica, the capital of the county, I did not have time to change from my everyday clothes to more presentable ones because I had to rush to a *Cyfarfod Dosbarth*[2] which was held in Prospect – a journey of 15 miles. I listened to the following ministers preaching the gospel: Richard Isaac, Iowa; E. C. Evans, Remsen; Thomas Evans, Holland Patent; D. M. Jones, Floyd and William A. Jones, Utica. These meetings are considered of minor importance, yet I felt that the preaching aspect, on this day, was as good as any held in Wales.

Welsh settlements in Oneida are amongst the oldest and most respected in the country. The people are mainly from north Wales and many of them have been in America for over forty years. Most of the inhabitants of the parishes of Steuben and Remsen speak the Welsh language, and even children, whose grandparents never lived in Wales, speak Welsh without any twang whatsoever. Most of the chapels in these areas are similar to the ones in Wales. However, in the towns of Utica and Rome, chapel-buildings have galleries and are very grand. At one time, there were as many as ten Welsh chapels in the parish of Remsen alone, whilst no other nation had any places of worship in the entire neighbourhood. A few English churches have since appeared. Dr Everett,[3] the famous editor of *Y Cenhadwr* lives on the outskirts of Remsen. He is very religious and is well-respected by the Union of Congregationalists. His children follow their father in the business of publishing *Y Cenhadwr*, which is a monthly periodical.

The majority of Welsh people living in Oneida are farmers. The fertile valley of the Mohawk River runs through the Welsh settlement. However, Welsh immigrants have left the more productive regions of the valley to the Americans whilst choosing the more hilly parts for themselves. The reason may be that the air is fresher in the upper region; and perhaps the hills remind them of the Old Country's landscape. In reality, it would be more profitable for Welsh settlers if they occupied lowland farms, especially now that the land is being tilled and cultivated – hence eliminating malaria and other unpleasant elements. I do understand that my compatriots, as well as immigrants from other countries, are beginning to follow the example of the English by now, and are opting for farmland in the valley.

The Welsh in Oneida seem to be quite comfortable with their environment and circumstances; most of them own farms and have well-built houses and outbuildings as well as very fertile land. Most land prices vary from 25 to 150 dollars per acre but land surrounding the towns can fetch as much as 600 dollars per acre. Dairy farming is the main occupation in this region and farmers transport milk to a cheese-producing plant. A farmer with a herd of twenty cattle takes about 600 pounds of milk daily to the factory; that amount of milk makes around 50 pounds of cheese. The whey is fed to the pigs. I understand that the inhabitants of Oneida have a more honourable opinion of the Welsh than that of some Londoners in England. According to rumour, water is added to milk by a few Welsh dairymen in London. Some have been fined for this practice over here but on the whole, everyone in the dairy business in this region is very honest.

On a 20–30 acre farm, about thirty cows, two or three horses, pigs and some other animals and poultry are kept. In some regions, the calves are culled when they are three days old; their meat is fed to dogs and their skins sold. The land in Oneida is used primarily for grazing with only a few crops grown.

Many Welsh people living in the southern part of Oneida County find work in hop harvesting. The roots are planted in the ground 7 or 8 feet apart. Long stakes are placed between each hop so that the branches cling to them at a height of 15 to 20 feet. Growth takes place around the middle of May and the blossom appears towards the beginning of July. It is harvest time when the petals on the cones start fading to brown. At the beginning of September, the branches are cut to a height of three feet above ground. The stakes and branches are afterwards removed before the hops are gathered and placed to dry above intense heat in a loft. About 1,200 pounds of hops are cultivated per acre but there is often a wide margin in prices. Some years they only fetch 10 cents per pound; other years they sell for around 30 cents. On average, prices are in the bracket of 20 cents per pound. The same roots can be used for planting for a period of ten years; thereafter they become too strong and are destroyed.

It is difficult, in some circumstances, to establish what is sinful and what is proper in this part of the country. It is not permissible for a brewer or a retailer of alcohol, and in some cases a drinker of alcohol, to be a church member here. Such people are considered unworthy members of society. Yet, many hop growers are judged by the church as honourable members of their communities. As far as I understand, hops have only one use, which is to produce alcoholic drinks. This has been a topic of discussion in Church Assembly Meetings and each time the matter is put forward, the ruling is that this livelihood is permissible. Church officials in Wales came to the same decision when the issue of Welsh people selling milk on a Sabbath in London was raised.

A settler who is unable to buy a farm in Oneida for financial reasons, can rent one for a sum of between two and ten dollars per acre, according to the value of the farm and condition of the soil. Others pay rent for animals, implements and the land whilst others buy their farms by instalments over several years. Some farm by a 'share' agreement. The farmer is responsible for the horses, implements and half of the cattle and gives a percentage of the produce to the land owner. In fact, various arrangements are drawn up between tenants and landlords. Although immigrants can still settle in Oneida, it is not advisable at present, since there is better land for less money towards the west.

---

[1] Calvinistic Methodists' Connection: a group of Methodist Ministers and Officials who meet to discuss matters of denominational importance.

[2] *Cyfarfod Dosbarth* (District Meeting): meeting of ministers and laymen, similar to a monthly meeting held by the Methodists in Wales.

[3] Dr Robert Everett (1791–1875) was editor of *Y Cenhadwr Americanaidd*. Born in Flintshire, Wales, he was ordained a minister with the Congregationalists at Capel Lôn Las, Denbigh in 1815. In 1823, he was called to take charge of the Welsh Religious Cause at Utica, New York.

4

Early Settlers; the Religious Press; Pen-y-Caerau, Coal-mining

It is interesting to listen to elderly people, who came to America with their parents when very young, narrating about their experiences in the forests. Divine wisdom is so clear in the Creation. Everything exists for a purpose and at a specific time. Sixty or more years ago, oppression and hardship in the Old Countries caused many to take risks by crossing the ocean to seek better living conditions here. The voyages at that time were long and uncomfortable and immigrants were prepared to accept any kind of terrain after landing. People preferred to suffer inconveniences and hardships in remote areas rather than contemplate a three-month return voyage over the perilous ocean. Their single-room dwellings, made of stocks and planks, could be spotted throughout the forests. The trees surrounding their cabins were felled in order to have a clearance to grow maize and potatoes between the stumps. Crops, animals and the production of milk served as the people's livelihood. The animals would roam and graze in the forests which had no boundaries whatsoever, yet they had an inner instinct telling them to return to their owners' home in the evenings. 'The ox knoweth his owner, and the ass his master's crib' (Isaiah 1:3).

Just in case something disrupted this routine at any time, a bell was attached to the oldest, wisest and most deserving cow – one which the others acknowledged as their chief. Brute animals recognise a leader amongst them and they adhere to the guidance of their boss with greater attention than that done by humans. Wherever the bell was heard ringing, that was always the spot where the animals were found gathered together. In the early days, oxen were used to pull the plough and haul various loads. People used to travel in big, heavy wagons during the summer and on sledges in winter to go to their places of worship. They could be heard approaching from quite a distance since the drivers had to shout at their oxen and crack their whips constantly to urge them on. The oxen would plod along, leaning against each other with solemn expressions and bowed heads as if they were counting their steps along the way.

Travellers of yesteryear would encounter obstacles like large potholes and drifting snow at times, yet they felt that the prayer meetings or sermons conducted by their dear preacher in the rented chapel were sufficient reward for all their difficulties, and they felt rejuvenated after attending a service. One horse would be shared by people in the communities and it was used mostly for urgent errands. Cereal crops would be taken to the mill to be ground – a distance of between 15 and 20 miles usually. When undertaking a journey, the farmer would take an axe with him and use it to cut notches on the trees en route. These indicators enabled him to find his way home on the same path that he had set out. Many strange and remarkable tales are told about the first settlers in Oneida and the surrounding district. Nowadays, the area has a different appearance; trees have been felled, land has been tilled, meadows are flourishing and the terrain has been divided into farms with large, beautiful buildings enhancing the landscape. Today, people who travel into towns, villages or to chapel meetings do so in light buggies in the summer and on comfortable sleigh-cars during wintertide. I shall explain it all to the people of Wales upon my return.

In a literary sense, the settlement in Oneida is the most important one of all the Welsh settlements in America. It is here that the main magazines and newspapers are being printed. *Y Cenhadwr*, the Congregationalists' monthly paper, is printed in Remsen; it was established and edited by the late Dr Everett who died in 1875; however, his children are continuing to run the business. In Utica *Y Cyfaill* is printed. This paper is older than *Y Cenhadwr. Y Cyfaill*, like *Y Drysorfa* in Wales, belongs to the Calvinistic Methodists. Its founder and patron for many years was the late Reverend W. Rowlands DD, but these days Reverend W. Roberts is the editor. *Y Wawr*, the Baptists' monthly paper, is also printed in Utica. This paper is only four years old and follows *Y Glorian* and *Seren Orllewinol* – papers which have been in distribution for many years. *Y Drych*, the oldest of the Welsh papers is also printed in Oneida. It is a very valuable newspaper for our nation in America.

Utica is the capital of Oneida, with a population of 37,000, but only a small sector contains Welsh people. Four railroads run through this urban area and there are four Welsh chapels of different denominations in the town. Rome, population 14,000, has three railroads and two Welsh chapels – Methodist and Congregational. Apart from the mentioned towns, there are numerous villages in the settlement where many Welsh people live. Most of Remsen's population of 600 are Welsh; Prospect has a population of 700; Holland Patent, population 500; Waterville, population 2,200. There are many Welsh people residing in different locations in Lewis County, an area north of Oneida. A percentage of the people living in Madison and Otsego counties are also Welsh.

One of the natural wonders of this part of the country is Trenton Waterfalls which is a magnet for many tourists every summer. Since it is too treacherous to go near it during wintertime because of snow and ice, I am unable to describe it since I did not have a close view, but by all accounts, it is very spectacular during the summer months.

When I was near Holland Patent, I met a Welshman from Pontrhydfendigaid, west Wales, Rees P. James, son of Daniel James, Dolebolion Farm and nephew of Morgan James, Glan-yr-afon. He came to this country as a young man in 1849. He married, had two children, bought a farm and built a large barn worth 2,300 dollars. Soon after the barn was completed and filled with the farm's produce and some implements, it was destroyed by fire. His wife and two children also died during this tragic time. Like Job he was thrown from plenty to poverty, yet in spite of all adversity, like Job again he forged ahead, remarried and rose to greater prosperity than before. His second wife hails from the Blaenannerch area of west Wales and is a relative of the Hughes Blaengader family. They have two children and I had the privilege of christening the younger one. Mr James and his family now live on a holding of 260 acres, keep fifty dairy cattle and do not owe a penny to anyone. I categorise him as one of the successful farmers of America.

Whilst many Welsh settlers prosper in this country, I must not forget other reports I have heard and I am obliged to point out the other side of the coin. Not everyone succeeds here; it is people who work hard by cultivating their land and improving their circumstances that do well in America: 'If any would not work, neither should he eat' (II Thessalonians 3:10). This quotation is more fitting here than in the Old Country since many over there do not make full use of their abilities or experiences, yet profit from the labour of those who do actually work, with the result that the workers very often do not have enough means to eat proper meals. It should not be this way; the system in every country should be: 'The hand of the diligent maketh rich' (Proverbs 10:4).

If an occasional week goes by without me addressing you[1] it will be because of my busy schedule. The Welsh settlements in this country are like the heaven's stars, appearing in the most unexpected places. To accomplish my objectives, I have to hurry from one settlement to another, enquire about people's past – both materialistic and spiritual. I like to find out about people's nationality and to what religious denomination they belong. I record the information and pass it on in my Letters to newspapers. Although my mission is to find out about the Welsh immigrants' circumstances in this country, they, on the other hand, are just as keen to find out from me about life in Wales. Between everything, I find that I am unable to find time to contribute to my column in *Y Faner* every week; however, I shall do my best not to miss out on too many instalments.

Before I move on from Oneida, I must report about Pen-y-caerau,[2] an old and respectable settlement 2 miles east of Remsen. Here one finds the oldest Welsh Methodist church in the settlement and a graveyard that is the Machpelah[3] of the denomination in the entire area. It was here that the bodies of the old pilgrims, ministers, deacons and so forth were buried. It was the wish of the old pioneers to be buried in this sacred graveyard. They felt that the most prestigious homage that could be bestowed on them was to have their final resting place at Pen-y-caerau's graveyard after their laborious life in this world. These folk encountered harsh times and withstood difficult circumstances, but their descendants inherited all of their splendid achievements and they have made sure

Pen-y-caerau Chapel

that their ancestors' names live on in high esteem.

Again, before I rush on to the coalmining area of Pennsylvania, I must point out that I should have said that *Eos Glan Twrch*[4], brother of Reverend D. Edwards, Newport, south Wales, lives in Rome. He is considered as an outstanding bard amongst the Welsh in America. Utica is the prime place for the main *eisteddfodau*[5] and the town is viewed as the Athens of the United States.[6]

On 28th December [1880] I left Utica for Scranton – a distance of about 150 miles. I had to travel through Norwich, Binghamton and other towns. The Welsh are not as numerous in Scranton as they used to be, although many do live in the surrounding area. Hyde Park is situated on the other side of the Lackawanna River and there are three Welsh chapels appertaining to three denominations in this town. The Congregationalists and the Baptists have 400 members each and the Calvinistic Methodists about

160; the Methodists do have another chapel in Bellevue, which is only a mile away from Hyde Park. Reverend Dr Roberts used to be in charge of Bellevue chapel, which is one of the most ornate chapels ascribed to the Welsh in America. However, I now understand, as I did when I was here nine years ago, that it is unused. On viewing the chapel from the outside, it appears full of splendour and apparently it is thus inside, but because of its vastness and inadequate heating system, it is more convenient to conduct most services in the basement. Although champions of their Cause, one could say that the Calvinistic Methodists, both in Bellevue and Hyde Park, are unfortunate as far as use of their chapels is concerned, especially during wintertide.

Many Welsh newspapers and magazines are printed in these urban areas and Hyde Park is classified next to Utica as far as Welsh literature is concerned. This area is also renowned for its *eisteddfodau* and other nationalistic events.

The first news I heard on my arrival in Hyde Park was that Reverend Joseph E. Davies DD, a minister whose company I much enjoyed on many occasions, had passed away after a long illness. Dr Davies was known as one of the most gifted Welsh theologians in the country. He published three volumes entitled *Y Blwch Diwinyddol*[7] as well as another book on different religious issues. He also contributed many articles to *Y Cyfaill* and other papers. Because of his honest, conscientious, easily understood method in all his duties, he probably did not get the publicity he would have had if he had adopted a different style. I trust that he is now in the land where the sky is cloudless and the light so clear that principles and objectives are understood and appreciated: 'For there shall be no night there' (Revelations 21:25).

In this region of Pennsylvania, one comes across the towns of Providence and Taylorville, where there are many Welsh people who regularly attend Welsh churches of different denominations. The Calvinistic Methodists are quite numerous in the agricultural regions – more so than in the mining areas; it is the Wesleyans who are strong amongst the Americans though.

The coalmining areas of Southern Pennsylvania are the largest and most prosperous in the country. Anthracite is the coal mined here and it is abundant in the counties of Carbon, Lackawanna, Luzerne, Schuylkill, Columbia, Northumberland and Dauphin with thousands of Welsh people living in these regions. People who are familiar with coalmining, in Wales as well as America, say that the methods used in America are more advanced than those in Wales. Every mine-proprietor in America is legally obliged to safeguard that enough air is circulating within the pits to make the Davy lamps[8] surplus to requirement, apart from special or unforeseen circumstances. The injected air is diverted into eight or ten different channels and it is quantified on a weekly basis. It is said that in the Pen-y-graig mine in south Wales, where a major accident took place recently, 70,000 cubic feet of air was circulating at the time of the disaster and this was considered to be acceptable. In this part of America, an average of 85,000 cubic feet of air per minute circulates for the benefit of less manpower than that in Wales, with the result that an accident is a rare occurrence here. Another contributory factor must be the hours worked by miners in America; they only work during daytime, whereas in Wales, it is a 24-hour shift system.

Many Welsh people who have connections with coalmining in this region have been promoted to high positions and are very affluent. Although many nationalities work in these mines, most of the senior posts have been allocated to the Welsh. At the moment, one cannot say that the industry is bustling. There are more people working in the mines than are actually required, with the consequence that not all of them are employed on a full-time basis. As far as I can gather, everyone does enjoy a fairly good standard of living; I have not heard anything to the contrary anyway. The prospect of a promotion is slight, although there are signs of better days on the horizon. The salary of an inspector is between 90 and 100 dollars per month; a miner earns in the region of two dollars daily, and a labourer one and a half dollars per day.

It was in Carbondale, on the north side of the coalfield, that the mining industry started in 1822. Carbondale (population 10,000) has many Welsh residents. Scranton, population 45,000; Pittston, 15,000, Wilkes-Barre, 25,000; Bloomsburg, 5,000; Danville, 11,000; Shamokin, 7,000; Ashland, 6000; Shenandoah, 9000; Mahanoy City, 8,000; Pottsville, 20,000; Hazleton, 8,000. All these towns, as well as others, have a large percentage of Welsh people living in them. Danville has other industries apart from coalmining, namely: several blast furnaces and three mills. Messrs William and David Williams, sons of the elderly deacon David J. Williams, are managers of two mills.

I met friends of mine from Stockton-on-Tees, England, in Danville. I had heard that they had left for America when I was over in Wales. I had also heard, at a monthly Methodist meeting in my home country, that these people had regretted their venture and that they would have returned, had they been in a position to do so. However, I was pleased to find that what was said to me at that meeting in Wales was just a false rumour. The men were in full-time employment; their homes were beautifully furnished and they owned expensive harmoniums. They were all well-dressed and their dining tables were full of delicacies. Although they had *hiraeth*[9] for their homeland, they very much resented the fact that people in Wales were suggesting that they were too poor to return to their native land.

When I started my objective of gathering information about my compatriots all over the United States of America, I was afraid that my suitability for the task would be in doubt, but as I journeyed on, all such apprehensions disappeared because I have had a warm welcome everywhere. My undertaking, although troublesome at times, is very enjoyable and rewarding. I am beginning to think that I belong to all the Welsh denominations as well as the two countries. Apart from the fact that I am accepted and appreciated by chapel-goers, I am given assistance regarding understanding the history of Welsh settlements in America and I have also been given many books and pamphlets by people who escort me. These publications enable me to research into specific elements relating to our nation in this country over many years. John Roberts, Remsen, gave me forty copies of *Cyfaill o'r Hen Wlad*; Mr Rees Herbert, Youngstown, Ohio, gave me thirty copies of *Y Cenhadwr Americanaidd* (the Congregationalists' monthly), and Lazarus Mathias, Mineral Ridge, Ohio, gave me several copies of *Y Seren Orllewinol*, *Y Glorian* and *Y Wawr*. I have also been given other interesting papers by friends in different localities. The different denominations co-operate well to ensure that I have a successful and rewarding journey. I hope that they will not be disappointed.

Every so often, I come across strange characters. In Carbondale, there lived an eccentric deacon by the name of William Maxi. He had never pursued graciousness and dignity although, eventually, he did have a change of heart. No doubt his character was affected by unpleasant experiences in his youth. He had a habit of passing judgement on a sermon, verbally as well as by grimaces, even when the preacher was delivering his message. He would utter, 'Oh – Hum – Indeed – Very good. Well – Well – Hum – Hum. Well, that will do – Yes, all right.' The late Reverend Howell Powell was held in high esteem by him. Reverend Powell was preaching in Carbondale once and the collection was being donated towards the upkeep of a particular chapel. The sermon was about Christ completing his work on earth and his redemption on the Cross. Powell was such a skilful preacher that Maxi forgot his usual mannerisms and comments and became all ears. The unexpected silence made the congregation think they were worshipping somewhere else!

The following day, Mr Powell and Reverend T. J. Phillips, who is a minister in Plymouth now, called on Maxi in order to collect his offering towards this specific chapel. He had just returned from his shift at the coalmine and was having a wash and a change of clothes. 'Well, Mr Maxi, I expect you know why we have called,' said Mr Powell.

'Yes, Mr Powell, I surely do,' said Maxi. 'Shonet,' Maxi called to his wife, 'Please pass my breeches – the ones on the staircase. There is a 5-dollar note in the pocket; go and change it and give half to Mr Powell.'

'There you are, Mr Phillips,' Powell remarked, 'This donation will contribute towards patching Jesus Christ's boots.' (Apparently, Powell had spoken metaphorically the previous evening about Jesus Christ having his feet still on the ground and that any contribution whatsoever towards the Cause would keep his feet comfortable.)

Maxi was so touched by this remark that he replied:

'*Diawst*, Shonet, give it all to him so that Christ can have a *new* pair of boots.'

I heard many stories about this amusing character but I have to continue with my mission.

[1] A reference to W. D. Evans's letters to the press.

[2] Pen-y-caerau (pen: peak; caerau: forts). The Calvinistic Methodists of Wales came to Steuben, New York state, early in 1800 and worshipped at the Union Church of *Capel Ucha* (*capel*: chapel; *ucha(f)*: upper) until they organized as a Congregational Society. It was then that the Methodists felt strong enough to have a church of their own. In 1824, Pen-y-caerau church was built. It was the first church organized and established by the Calvinistic Methodists in America.

[3] *Machpelah*: Hebrew word for Tomb of the Patriarchs.

[4] *Eos Glan Twrch*: bardic name of John Edwards (1806–1887), poet and prose writer.

[5] *Eisteddfodau*: Welsh festivals of competitions in poetry, singing and reciting.

[6] Athens of the United States: comparison to Athens as the leading city of ancient Greece.

[7] *Y Blwch Duwinyddol* (The Theological Box) was published in Scranton, Pennsylvania between 1867 and 1871)

[8] The Davy Lamp was devised by Sir Humphry Davy in 1815. Sir Humphry (1778–1829) was an English chemist.

[9] *Hiraeth*: Welsh word for 'longing'.

5

More Slate-works; Philadelphia; Wilkes-Barre; Delaware

After passing through the mining areas, I arrived again in a slate-quarrying region which has its centre-point, I believe, at Slatington, Pennsylvania. It is said that this region produces the best slate in the world for use as writing supplies in schools. I went to the factories to see the slates being manufactured and it is amazing how swift and easy the whole process of constructing and framing can be. Many Welsh people live in this area and they appear to be prosperous and responsible in their occupations and activities. The quarrymen of Vermont apply the same method as that used in Northampton and Lehigh when constructing slates. At one time, there were churches by three Welsh denominations in this region. Nowadays, only Methodists and Congregationalists hold services here. The outlook, as far as the continuation of Welsh ministering in this patch is concerned, is rather gloomy, although it should not be so in my opinion.

Most of the slate quarrymen are north-Walians, immaterial where they reside, whereas the coalminers are usually south-Walians. The quarries are to be found in the counties of Northampton and Lehigh on the eastern side of the state. During last year, 30,000 boxes of framed slates were produced with approximately 150 in each box. Last year's numbers were less than that of the previous year by 6,000 boxes. As far as roofing slates were concerned, 9,000 more were constructed than in the preceding year. The first buildings were constructed in Slatington in 1851. Today, it is a town of 2,500 inhabitants. The Welsh people who live here are fluent in three languages: Welsh, English and German. The youngsters find Welsh the most difficult with German the easiest.

Thereafter, I went to Philadelphia – the city of the first Welsh settlers. Their descendants are 100 per cent American by now. After entering Montgomery County, near Philadelphia, I noticed farm buildings resembling those in Wales. Some had skylights and some of these outbuildings had been built facing the front of houses with straw stacks separating them from the dwellings. The countryside looked impressive – a vast undulating landscape as far as the eye could see. This area, which used to be forested, is now beautiful countryside and you will not find more respectable people than the descendants of the Welsh settlers who live here. The name of one railroad station is North Wales; another is Gwynedd and another Penllyn. Farther on, one finds the Jenkin and Pencoed railroad stations. That is the pattern throughout this region with towns, villages and railroad stations having Welsh names, whilst many of the residents have surnames such as Williams, Davies, Roberts, Evans, Jones and so forth.

Philadelphia is the old city of William Penn,[1] who was a descendant of a Welshman from Penmynydd, Anglesey. It is the second city in America as far as importance and influence are concerned and it has a population of around 1,000,000. Many of the residents are Welsh people who have a great deal of influence on the development of the city as well as the entire state of Pennsylvania. Many of my kinfolk have held responsible positions in this region. The city of Philadelphia is clean and orderly and no other city can claim such high standards as far as religion and morality are concerned. The Welsh influence was very strong here at one time and there used to be a splendid, well-attended

Welsh chapel in the city. I see no reason why this situation should not be so again.

From Philadelphia, I went to West Bangor – a distance of about 100 miles. Slate quarrying is the main occupation of the men of this town and the method used is almost the same as that in Wales. Roof slates are constructed here and the workings are managed at the face of the rock. Lead is a component of these slates which is why they are strong and retain their dark blue colour. They are usually sold for 5 dollars per square. These quarries are owned by Welshmen such as John Humphreys from Corris, William Parry from Llanberis, Ebenezer Jones and Robert Jones from Ffestiniog and others. There used to be three Welsh denominations here – Wesleyan, Congregational and Calvinistic Methodist. The Wesleyans have already ceased to hold services; the Congregationalists are weak but the Methodists are doing well under the ministerial guidance of Reverend Edward J. Hughes. He is a native of Corris, north Wales, and is held in high esteem by everyone.

To go to and from West Bangor, I had to wade across the Susquehanna River. This splendid river flows down from the Allegheny Mountains. The last time I saw it, it was summer and the scene was of clear water forming frothy cascades as it rushed down over rocks on its way to the ocean. The Susquehanna is not suitable for navigation, although during summertime it is used to convey trees by rafts to various markets. About 100 of these logs are tied together, end to end, and on the last attachment there is a small cabin with three or four men attending to the wood in order to ensure easy passage between the islands. When they reach waterfalls, the men all rush to the rear end of the ferry, after they have made sure that the rafts are in the best position for the drop over the falls. The whole process looks as if a very long snake is slithering along. When the last attachment reaches the dip, the men make sure that they hold on to something to avoid any accidents.

There are impressive buildings and good farmland on the islands of this river and the residents are almost self-sufficient inasmuch as they have the benefit of the produce from their farms, and access to any amount of fish and birds, of course. I would think that the only drawback is the hazard of flooding at times.

I travelled on to Wilkes-Barre, where there are many Welsh people residing, with religion thriving amongst them. Here, one finds the most popular Methodist church in the state of Pennsylvania. Its minister is Reverend Thomas B. Thomas, a native of Aberaeron and a nephew of the late Reverend Abel Green. I had the opportunity of being in a theological meeting in this church and I found it to be one of the most organised and systematic I had ever attended. In the absence of the minister, John Griffiths, one of the deacons, presided. Mr Griffiths is a very honourable man and was a conscientious manager in the coal industry for many years; unfortunately he sustained a serious injury and is unable to fulfil that post now. His position, at present, is County Treasurer of a society that adheres to parliamentary regulations. I was surprised to find that everyone understood the rules at this meeting. A resolution to establish a church in a nearby location was passed and certain people were appointed to go to Wilkes-Barre to instruct the branch as to the method of progression. Other issues were discussed but no time was wasted and this part of the meeting was over in good time; this break enabled us to discuss spiritual concerns. Deputations to church meetings in Wales could learn from people of this faraway land about making good use of surplus time.

After the meeting was over, my friend Morgan Williams, from Llanbadarn Fawr near Aberystwyth, and I were on our way to a guesthouse when we heard the sound of a religious service in a nearby building. We proceeded to investigate and since we could see that people were still arriving, we only ventured to the doorway. We decided to sit near the entrance but were warmly welcomed and therefore moved nearer the pulpit because we were anxious to hear and see all that was taking place. We soon realised that we were at one of the Negroes' revival meetings. It is a custom with these people to welcome other worshippers to join them every winter in such services, irrespective of denomination, colour or creed.

Whatever you, Welsh people, think about people designating certain times for the Lord's work, these people believe that some services should be allocated to wintertime and they say to the Lord: 'Keep this ordinance in its season from year to year' (Exodus 13:10). I know some people make light of such occurrences but maybe we should not be too hasty to pass judgement. The fowler goes to places where most birds are gathered and the angler follows his calling according to the proper season. Evangelists are the people's fishermen and they have to be as astute as serpents, and at the same time, as innocuous as doves. Paul, the apostle, purposely did not cut himself off from the wiles and cunning of certain people so that, ultimately, he could convert such persons away from their evil ways. Dwight Moody,[2] one of the greatest evangelists of this century, also ensures that everything possible is attained for the well-being of people in places of worship. He makes sure that churches and chapels are well-lit and properly heated in winter. If only a few people are present at certain services, he tells them to close up to one another. I wish Moody would visit Wales at wintertime to hear people's teeth rattling when congregations are shivering in chapels and churches. I do not know why places of worship are not heated in winter in my home country but one preacher is known to have prophesised that no one with cold feet is capable of being saved! The shortest sermon can seem endless and the most melodious preacher can appear dull when the congregation is enduring very low temperatures.

I am going off-track now, though. I should be with the Negroes at this time and not with conditions back in Wales. What I am proclaiming is: we should make use of all amenities to make life more comfortable for Christ's followers. People in this part of the country have more time to attend places of worship during the winter than at other times of the year and the Negro preachers consider it wise to focus on this theory and impress this notion on people's minds. When Daniel foresaw that his people were about to be liberated: 'He went into his house; and his windows being open in his chamber toward Jerusalem, he kneeled upon his knees three times a day, and prayed, and gave thanks before his God, as he did aforetime' (Daniel 6:10). These Negro people have proved many a time that the Lord leans towards them every winter; therefore, they increase their commitment to pray and instruct their members to double their devotion. When Methodist meetings are held in Wales, procedures are very orderly, but order was not an important factor in this service.

The Welsh people of Wilkes-Barre should be recognised for the admirable work they do in the community. Reverend D. H. Williams is one worthy of mention. It was in this town that I came across the lectress Mrs Roberts from Iowa. Her subjects are astronomy and geology and I have heard that she is an authority in both fields.

From Cleveland, I had to travel for more than 100 miles to Delaware – a town of around 8,000 inhabitants. Important sulphur wells are located in this neighbourhood and are of great attraction to many visitors. For the benefit of Welsh people, there is a small Congregational church in Delaware under the supervision of Reverend John H. Jones. The Ohio Wesleyan University is also here, and it was in this college I studied for two years in order to prepare myself for the ministry. There are many prominent Welshmen in this town – people like the Honourable J. P. Powell, who is a much respected lawyer; Judge J. S. Jones; and Professor Williams and his late wife had Welsh ancestors. Mrs Williams was a sister of the Davies doctors of Cincinnati. She was a Welsh lady through and through. Mr Merick, the Chancellor of the University until recently, claimed that he was also a descendant of a Welsh family by the name of Meurig and for that matter, as far as appearance can be taken into account, he could not relate to any other nationality!

---

[1] William Penn (1644–1718), Quaker founder of the province of Pennsylvania.

[2] Dwight Lyman Moody (1837–1899) was an American evangelist and publisher who founded the Northfield Schools in Massachusetts, the Moody Church and Moody Bible Institute in Chicago.

6

Radnor; Columbus; Bryniau Cymru; Youngstown; Palmyra; Cleveland

Eight miles north of Delaware, lies the parish and village of Radnor. They were named thus by the first settlers who arrived in the area from Radnorshire at the beginning of the nineteenth century, and both Congregationalists and Methodists have established Welsh churches here. Agriculture is the main industry in the region owing to its rich, arable land. The people who are farming here are quite prosperous and land fetches a high price. The area is renowned for its working horses and many stallions are brought over from as far as Wales and Europe. The Congregational chapel of Troedrhiwdalar[1] is situated between Radnor and Delaware; its name is another reminder of where the first settlers to this region came from.

Because I was in this area, I decided to visit my brother John and his family. They have all integrated into the American way of life and have a warm affection towards their neighbours and church. John is of the opinion that it is a very narrow-minded attitude to think that worshipping amongst English-speakers is not gratifying. I, myself, also had a realisation that I should be more religious and open-minded.

When I arrived with my relatives, they were in the process of making maple syrup (or maple treacle, as it is known by some). The maple syrup camp is in a forest of many tall, beautiful trees. During the month of March, a notch is made in the lower part of the trees – just three inches above the ground. From this notch, a sweet sap flows through elder-wood pipes into vessels which have been placed in certain places to contain it. This process takes several days to complete. Barrels are taken to the camp every day and the liquid from the vessels is poured into them. This sweet sap is then boiled until it thickens into a treacly consistency. In my opinion, this treacle is the best on the market, but I do not remember tasting it when I was in Wales.

Whilst I was staying with my brother and sister-in-law, I came across very strange stone tools which had been dug from the ground and had belonged to Red Indians at one time. If possible, I shall take them back with me and donate them to the museum at Aberystwyth University.

I continued my journey to Columbus, the capital of Ohio – population 40,000. It was here, early in 1868, that I started preaching the gospel. I have fond memories of that time and of the warm welcome I received by church members. I am so glad to find that this church is still flourishing under the ministerial guidance of Reverend R. V. Griffiths. There is also a Welsh Congregational Church in the city under the ministry of Reverend J. Jones, a native of Penllyn, north Wales.

Newark was my next destination, a place where I spent several years of my childhood. Newark has a population of around 9,000, with many Welsh people residing in the town and surrounding countryside. The Welsh have two churches in this town – Congregational and Calvinistic Methodist. The Congregationalists are without a minister at present, but the Methodists have Reverend Thomas Roberts, formerly of Ysbyty Ifan, north Wales, as their minister. He is very much respected and his ministry is a blessing to the Cause. Reverend E. J. Evans, whose son is Dr Llewelyn Ioan Evans of Lane's Theological Institute, Cincinnati, also lives in Newark. Reverend Evans was minister of the Welsh Methodist Church here in Newark for many years. Although he is retired now, he is always ready to help out, if need be.

Three miles from Newark, one finds the oldest of the Welsh settlements in these regions, namely Bryniau Cymru (the hills of Wales). The first white person to settle here was a Welshman who was known as Dafydd Tomos Mawr. Very interesting tales have been told about this man. During the American Revolutionary War[2], when he was a youngster, he used to live in Philadelphia. A young, engaged couple came over from Wales to America at that time. Unfortunately, the young man was kidnapped by the 'press gang'[3] to serve as a soldier in the English army. The girl then made her way to Philadelphia and she and her fiancé communicated by letters. However, Dafydd Domos[4] became acquainted with the girl and took a liking to her. By some unexplained means, letters from the fiancé stopped arriving and according to rumour, Dafydd Domos was collecting the girl's mail and destroying the letters from the soldier. After waiting for a letter from her fiancé for over two years, the girl came to the conclusion that the love of her life had been killed and she became closer to Dafydd Domos. She married him and after the war ended, they moved west to a very remote area and lived like Indians in a wigwam. Zanesville, 25 miles east, was the nearest township to their residence. They were amongst an Indian community who smoked tobacco habitually. Maize was ground between two stones by these people and each family kept a cow; their subsistence consisted mostly of milk and maize. This entire region is now known as Bryniau Cymru.

A cow went missing one Sunday morning and Dafydd Domos walked through the woods to see if he could find it.

Suddenly, he heard a strange noise – a kind of orchestral music as if a crowd was in a festive mood. At first, he believed he was hearing angels. He proceeded nearer the sound and after reaching a hillcrest, he saw a gathering of white people holding a religious service. As he approached these folk, they were amazed to see him and he, himself, was absolutely delighted since he had been bereft of companionship for such a long time. Hence, after this chance meeting, people from Wales and other countries settled in this location. When these settlers made their way to the shops and mill in Zanesville, they had to be extra vigilant because of the presence of wolves and bears in the woods.

After many years passed, who should come knocking on the door of Dafydd Domos and his wife one evening to ask for 'bed and breakfast' but the wife's former fiancé. He had survived the war, and of course much time had lapsed and old wounds had somewhat healed, with the consequence that the evening was spent jesting about old times and the parting was amicable the following morning.

The Baptist church in Bryniau Cymru was the first Christian church in the region. Its services were initially in Welsh but nowadays they are conducted in English. Bryniau Cymru's Methodist church was established many years after the Baptist one and the services are in Welsh to this day by this denomination. The village of Granville, west of Zanesville, is situated in a delightful location and contains two Welsh churches.

My next decision was to go 40 miles south to the towns of Shawnee and New Straitsville. These communities were only small villages ten years ago but the population has grown and only 3 miles separate them today. Coalmining is the attraction for settlers from Wales and several Welsh churches, affiliated to different denominations, have been established in these two towns. There are several taverns in these urban areas but the roads are quite muddy; however, I am sure that within a few years, the entire neighbourhood will have a better appearance.

The Western Reserve is in eastern Ohio and has been given this name because the land was designated for use by the army during the Revolutionary War, which took place between the years 1775 and 1783. The terrain has been divided into townships composed of sections and these sections dissected again into quarters. Every township is 5 miles long and likewise in width, therefore, 30 square miles comprises a piece of land measuring 640 acres. Every section is divided into four farms of 160 acres each, and a farm was given to every soldier who had served his full term in the army, or to relatives of servicemen who had died in action. Roads cross each other separating division from division. These roads run straight from east to west and from north to south, with crossroads at the end of every mile. In the middle of each township there is a village that has the same name as the town with the addition of the word 'centre'; for example, a village situated in the Palmyra Township is called Palmyra Centre. A 'village centre' is situated at the end of every 5 miles. This arrangement regarding land allotment is also adopted in the western states. I have little to report about certain towns in this location, namely: Brookfield, Coalburg, Hubbard and Crabtree. The entire area is linked to coalmining with many Welsh people living and working in them. The Congregationalists and Baptists have several Welsh chapels in the towns with the Calvinistic Methodists having one church in Brookfield.

I proceeded from the Western Reserve to Youngstown – a lively town which has grown in size, population and importance since I was a minister here twelve years ago. It has eight rolling mills, several blast furnaces and other important industries. As yet, I have not come across many familiar people in these parts, but Welsh religious services seem to be thriving, especially now that Reverend William Hughes of Wisconsin is a minister here. Mr Hughes is from north Wales originally and, unless I am mistaken, he used to be a minister in Llanrwst. The Baptist chapel is ministered by Venerable David Probert who established the denomination here around thirty years ago. At the moment, the Congregationalists are seeking an energetic minister to take charge of them. Reverend D. S. Davies, Bangor, used to be their minister. Several changes have taken place in nearby Church Hill and Weathersfield since my last stay in these towns. I used to be a minister in these communities as well as officiating in a chapel in Youngstown. It was nice to see familiar faces and I shall not forget their welcome this time round. Coalmining is the main industry in both locations but in Girard and Milestone, other neighbouring towns, there are many Welsh people working in mills and furnaces.

I had to travel a distance of 20 miles to go to Palmyra, an area where agriculture is the main industry, apart from the presence of one or two small coalmines. This district consists of an old Welsh settlement; a man by the name of John Davies, Bryncesyg, Cardiganshire, and his family, were the first to arrive here. They came in 1831 and soon afterwards, many Welsh families (from south Wales mostly) followed. The English had settled in the area a quarter of a century beforehand, therefore they had paved the way for the Welsh who, fortunately, did not have to confront Indians or wild beasts. There used to be a Welsh Unitarian chapel in this region and, as far as I know, it was the only one in America. It closed down several years ago and the

Calvinistic Methodists purchased the chapel. The first chapel in Palmyra belonged to the Congregationalists but the Methodist movement started soon afterwards. At first, the Methodists met in a chapel 3 miles outside the Centre, which meant they had to travel quite a distance to Sunday morning services. In order to stay for the afternoon meetings, they would bring baskets full of food and convene by a nearby well, which they used to quench their thirst. It was said that entanglements of black snakes and an occasional rattle one used to keep watch over the well during the summer months. Apparently, on Sundays, these snakes would move away from the water. Maybe, they feared the people who assembled there or else they were obeying their own Master who could be instructing them to give way to their superiors! It was said that after everyone had gone home, the serpents would return to the site of the well to eat the crumbs.

After so many years, members of this Methodist chapel thought it would be more appropriate to move the building into the village. After positioning it on a trailer, it started its slow journey towards the Centre. After reaching the brow of the hill, they realised that the cargo was too wide to cross a narrow bridge; they therefore, had to return to the nearest crossroads and there the chapel stayed as a place of worship for several more years. Nowadays, three Welsh denominations have comfortable chapels in the village. It was in this location, I met the bard Morddal Evans, and the two brothers, John R. and David R. Davies from Penuwch, Cardiganshire. The three of them are honourable deacons.

I went from Palmyra to nearby Parisville, where Reverend David Davies (*Dewi Emlyn*)[5] lives. He is well-known by Welsh people in America. Good land has been cultivated in this region and the Welsh farmers seem to be quite prosperous. The land is neither hilly nor flat but can be described as 'rolling', and a variety of crops is grown on the farmland, but I understand that livestock husbandry is the area's main enterprise. Land is sold from 50 to 100 dollars per acre.

After a journey of 30 miles, my next destination was Tallmadge, a place where coalmines are surrounded by beautiful countryside. I stayed in John W. Morris' home. He owned a small farm of 55 acres and the house and outbuildings were well-kept. The price of land here is 100 dollars per acre. Mr Morris' farm was valued at 5,500 dollars. I do not think that his implements, animals, and other chattels were very valuable, but to farm successfully in America one needs fewer animals and less manpower than that required in Wales. Comparison between the freedom and comfort which Mr Morris experiences on this small farm in America to that of a farmer in a similar situation in Wales is quite considerable.

Eight miles farther south, I found myself in the village of Thomastown, a place named after Mr Llywelyn Thomas, a miner who still lives in the locality. There are gentry living in this area and I have seen their mansions. I was both delighted and surprised to find that the village had been named after a Welsh miner rather than after someone who lived in a mansion. Coalmining is the occupation of the Welsh in this district and the Congregational denomination is the predominant one in Tallmadge and Thomastown. Both villages have comfortable chapels. Akron, a large town, is situated nearby and many Welshmen are occupied in its smelting works, but there are no Welsh religious services held in this town.

From, this region, I travelled 30 miles north to Newburgh and Cleveland – places situated on the banks of Lake Erie.

Cleveland is one of the main cities in America and between it and Newburgh, there are many Welsh people residing. Two brothers from Newburgh established the ironworks and today it is one of the largest industries in the state of Ohio. There are several mills and furnaces in these neighbourhoods, and Welsh religious services are held by three denominations in Newburgh. The Calvinistic Methodists' chapel is on the west side of the town.

A Welshman, one should never forget when mentioning Cleveland, is Samuel Job, a preacher affiliated to the Baptist Union. He is very broad-minded and is always doing all he possibly can to help his compatriots. He charges very little for preaching the Gospel and does all kinds of favours, immaterial of people's denomination or political preference. In appreciation of his services, he has been appointed by the city's leaders to be Chief Superintendent of Cleveland Bethel Home. This residence is a refuge for homeless sailors and others who are in the process of seeking work and so forth. Mr Job provides food, clothing and firewood to needy people and helps them to read and write. He took me to a hall where young girls were learning needlework. Dozens of pupils were there and they were supervised by several teachers. There was a very pleasant and Christian atmosphere in this classroom.

---

[1] Troedrhiwdalar in Wales is near Llanwrtyd Wells.

[2] The Revolutionary War in America, otherwise known as The American War of Independence (1775–1783): a change from the condition of British Colonies to national independence effected by the thirteen States of the American Union in 1776.

[3] Press-ganging: an act of forced conscription into military service, used most commonly in the nineteenth century.

[4] Dafydd Domos – The Tomos has become 'Domos' colloquially.

[5] *Dewi Emlyn*: Reverend David Davies (1817–1888), born at Pant-y-garn, Cenarth, Carmarthenshire. He began to preach in 1843, emigrated with his wife to the USA in 1852, and the same year was ordained at Paris, Portage, Ohio.

7

First Welsh Settlers; Ebensburg; Johnstown

It has been mentioned previously that the Welsh institutions in Oneida were among the oldest in the country as far as Welsh-speaking settlements were concerned. Welsh people moved from Philadelphia as far back as 1796 and there are many tales about the adventures of the first settlers who pressed ahead, in spite of perils and difficulties, to build homes for themselves on the wild and forested slopes of the Allegheny mountain range. Often they would have to sleep alongside their cargo in woods and were often disturbed by wild animals. Members of one family chose to sleep under cover of thick branches from a fallen tree one evening. When dawn broke, they found themselves covered by snow which had provided an extra layer to keep them warm for at least one night!

These eighteenth-century settlers, after reaching the area where Ebensburg is situated today, built makeshift homes for themselves and suffered a great deal of hardship because they were deprived of the basic necessities that would have made life more bearable for them. One man is reported to have started a journey of 22 miles to a mill, with a sack of corn on his back. At one point, he had to walk over a plank that was used to cross a stream, but as he was doing so the plank turned on its side and both man and sack fell into the water. The sack of corn was washed away by the flow but the man managed to reach the bank. He swore that it would have been better if he was dead rather than alive. He did live for many years after that unfortunate event and experienced more favourable living conditions in his latter years. Another tale records a couple who were in a camp boiling sap from a maple tree in order to make syrup, when on glancing upwards, they saw a bear sitting on a branch above them. Whilst the man ran indoors to fetch a gun and other weapons, the bear came down, but luckily, before it had a chance to attack the wife, she had grabbed a spade and given the beast such a blow that she broke its spine. When the husband reappeared, he found the defeated animal on its back on the ground.

A Welsh religious Cause was started in Ebensburg in 1797, in a place called Beulah – 3 miles from where Ebensburg is now. Reverend Morgan Rhys, a Baptist minister, was in charge of this movement. However, it was Reverend George Roberts, or Judge Roberts, as he was often referred to, who was hailed as foster-father in the settlement. Although he was a minister of religion, he was also an Associate Judge, and he is remembered as being a very fair judge, a successful peacemaker as well as a devout and conscientious minister. He was a brother of Reverend John Roberts, Llanbrynmair.

There is a tale about a man who had heard of Judge Roberts and had decided to pay him a visit. After reaching Roberts' neighbourhood, he came across a rather short man who was chopping wood, and he enquired, 'Where does Judge Roberts live?'

'He lives over there,' the wood-cutter replied. 'I shall come along to show you.'

They walked towards a certain house; the wood-cutter opened the door and both men entered and took a seat. After some general conversation, the visitor asked: 'Will Judge Roberts arrive shortly?'

'I am Judge Roberts,' replied the man – to the visitor's great amazement, since he had not expected to see a judge chopping wood.

Judge Roberts never finished a conversation with anyone

without mentioning the important factor of the soul. He was the minister in charge of the Congregational church. About forty years ago, the Calvinistic Methodists arrived from Wales and other countries to occupy land in this area and since they went into the trouble of travelling 6 miles north of the town of Ebensburg to worship, Reverend Roberts advised them to build a chapel of their own in Ebensburg. 'We are poor and cannot afford an undertaking like that,' was their answer.

'Come to us and we shall help you,' was Roberts' reply. The Methodists accepted this offer and collected 100 dollars, whilst the Congregationalists added another 225 dollars towards the project, with the result that a comfortable chapel was built in the town without delay. The Congregational church acted as a compassionate mother to the Methodists, and Reverend Roberts spread his wings to take charge of both denominations.

Nowadays, the Baptists conduct their worship in English, although it is the Welsh and descendants of former Welsh immigrants who frequent these services. The Congregationalists are the most numerous in this region but by now, more and more services are being conducted in English, rather than Welsh, by this denomination also. The Methodists are the ones holding on to services in Welsh, although not completely. The minister of the Methodist church is Reverend J. Islwyn Hughes. He has just returned from a visit to Wales and is much respected as a minister.

Ebensburg is situated high up on one of the Allegheny ranges and all the surrounding land is steep and rugged. There is nothing exceptional about the buildings in this region and the best-kept farms can be bought for about 20 dollars per acre. The farmers add lime and manure to the land, the same as is done in Wales. Different kinds of corn[1] and fruit are grown here, mostly for the purpose of animal fodder. There are some coalmines in the vicinity and lime is also quarried. Butter sales bring in a certain amount of income to the inhabitants of the region, but the main occupations are in the treatment of soot and the construction of staves and hoops for assembling barrels, tubs and suchlike. Although this area is not rich in natural resources, most of the farmers are freeholders, and through diligence and frugality have become quite affluent. It was here I came across Daniel Jones, brother of Reverend Joseph Jones, Ffosyffin, west Wales. The large town of Johnstown is situated about 18 miles south-west of Ebensburg. Iron and steel mills, blast-furnaces and coalmines are the main industries in this wide area. Many Welsh people are amongst Johnstown's population of 20,000 and three Welsh churches, of different denominations, have been established here.

---

[1] In the UK, 'corn' is a collective word for crops such as barley, wheat and oats; in the USA it is particularly used for maize.

8

Pittsburgh; Coal-mining; Salt-works; 'The Cardinganshire of America'

From Johnstown, I went to Pittsburgh, the most renowned city in the entire country for tin, iron and copper works. An engineer living in the city was reported to have said: 'If all the mills, blast-furnaces and other industrial buildings associated with the town of Pittsburgh were lined up, they would measure at least 36 miles.' Pittsburgh is separated from Allegany City by the Allegheny River and from South Side by the Monongahela River. These two rivers merge to form the Ohio River. Many Welsh people reside in Pittsburgh, which has a population of about 156,000. The Honourable Miles S. Humphreys lives here and is a member of the State's Legislature. Isaac Jones, a native of Cardiganshire, was an important figure in many circles within the city at one time and George Lewis, who hailed from Merthyr Tudful, his brothers and sons were amongst the founders of the rolling-mills industry in the country. There are numerous other Welsh people I could name who have been prominent members of society in Pittsburgh. The town has three Welsh churches and another in nearby, South Side; the latter is supervised by the Congregationalist minister, J. Gwawfryn Evans. Venerable Thomas Edwards, who was a Congregationalist minister in Cincinnati for many years, lives in South Side. Although Mr Edwards is advanced in years by now, he makes himself useful and is well respected in the neighbourhood. The Congregational church in Pittsburgh is under the ministry of Dr Thomas. The Baptist minister is Reverend A. J. Mortimer and the

Calvinistic Methodists are taken care of by both Dr Thomas and Reverend T. C. Davies. Both men have homes 6 miles outside Pittsburgh, where they can enjoy country air as well as having the benefit of amenities available in the nearby city. *Y Wasg*,[1] a Welsh publication, is printed in Pittsburgh.

From Pittsburgh, I went to Sharon – about 60 miles north-west of Pittsburgh. There are many rolling-mills in this town and coalmines in the surrounding area. I met Reverend Thomas Jenkins (Congregationalist) here; he is a native of Aberdare, and has translated into Welsh a book by Reverend James W. Dale entitled *Bedydd Clasurol* [Classical Baptism].[2] The Welsh people of Sharon were on top form the day I was there, since they had been victorious in an election the previous day. They had been successful in their support of Reverend Thomas Thomas, a Baptist minister and a native of Llangynog, Carmarthenshire. Mr Thomas had been appointed a magistrate and another Welshman, John Devereaux, had been elected as Town Councillor. Congratulations to both.

I arrived in New Straitsville and had about 100 miles of railroad track to cover to go to Gomeroy, a town on the banks of the Ohio – a river with an Indian name. The source of the Ohio is below Pittsburgh where the Allegheny and the Monongahela rivers merge. These two rivers also have Indian names, as do many place-names in this country. The Ohio River flows for hundreds of miles, with many streams and rivers pouring their waters into it along its journey before it reaches the outskirts of Cairo, Illinois, where it joins the Mississippi. It was the Ohio which separated the free states from the slave states during the enslavement period, and many a slave expressed immense relief after crossing this river; it is the largest tributary, by volume, of the Mississippi River. I myself do not find anything more spectacular regarding the Ohio, this time round, than when I sailed on it previously, except for sightings of large steamboats puffing back and forth on its waters. Some of these vessels resemble floating mansions; others, not so lavish, have floating containers, full of coal and other commodities, attached to them.

Pomeroy is the largest of a 7-mile string of towns on the north side of the Ohio River. South of Pomeroy lie Minersville, Syracuse and other villages, whilst Middleport is to the west. These communities are surrounded by steep hills, from which coal of the best quality is mined. One enterprise complements the other in this region: for instance, coal is extracted from the hills and then quickly transported into boats that take it downstream on the Ohio and its tributaries for hundreds of miles to different locations. The coalmines and the river are inter-dependent as far as employment is concerned, and the adjacent long plain is used for the construction of houses for the inhabitants of the area.

Apart from coalmines, there are between twenty and thirty saltworks in this district; some of them owned by companies from Wales. Salt is produced here from briny water which is drawn up hundreds of feet from the earth's depths, by means of pumps which are operated by steam-power. I shall do my best to describe the process here. The brine is sucked from the earth into a large container measuring 50 feet long and 25 feet wide. As the liquid settles in the container, a film of thick oil appears on the surface, similar to the way cream sets on milk. This oil, which is actually petroleum, is so profitable in Pennsylvania that it is considered a very valuable trading commodity in the state. To produce salt, the residual liquid is poured into large boilers so that the heating process can take place. High heat produces fine salt while low heat produces coarse salt. Twelve hours of fast boiling results in very fine salt, whilst five or six days on low heat produces the coarsest salt on the market. Firstly, the salt appears like snowflakes on the surface of the liquid before it becomes heavy and sinks to the bottom of the container. This sediment is removed and placed in a suitable room to dry for a few days; thereafter, it is ready to be deposited into barrels.

Since there are numerous saltworks in the region and therefore a need for barrels to contain the merchandise, many coopers are engaged here. One cooper can make about fifteen barrels in a day and there are many people earning a living by this occupation. Those who are proficient in cooperage should consider this area as a place of employment. Bromine is also processed in this location. It is, in fact, a by-product of salt and is produced from the liquid that is left in the containers after the salty sediment is removed. It is used by pharmacists, doctors and people of similar professions. The fumes which emitted from the method of developing this red liquid were so offensive that I could only stay to observe for a short while; therefore, I am unable to elaborate further on this topic.

One also finds smelting-works and one rolling-mill in this part of Ohio, although the mill is not in operation at present. Many Welshmen are in high positions as merchants here and two worthy of mention are the brothers Evan and David Edwards who are natives of Nantglyn, Denbighshire. I believe that they are relatives of Reverends Henry and William Rees and the famous *Twm o'r Nant*.[3] The Edwards brothers came to America with their parents and it seems that they are succeeding with issues relating to the two worlds![4] Ebenezer Williams, from Dowlais, South Wales, is a manager in the coal-mining industry and a worthy deacon in the Calvinistic Methodist church in Minersville. The

Honourable Alban Davies, a former member of the State Legislature, lives in Pomeroy. These are only a few of the prominent Welsh people who live in this region.

There are several Welsh churches of different denominations on each side of the Ohio River, and the Latter Day Saints[5] have a small church in Syraenae. In Middleport, Reverend Davies is a minister with the Campbellites[6] (or Disciples, as they like to be called) and Reverend Thomas Lloyd Hughes, son of the Honourable Thomas Ll. Hughes, Oak Hill, is in charge of the English Presbyterians in Pomeroy. He is young and handsome and one of the country's most notable scholars.

From Pomeroy, I went to Gallipolis where, in the 40s of this century, Welsh immigrants would disembark from their boats and make their way to settlements north of the Ohio River. Nowadays, only a few Welsh people reside in Gallipolis, therefore I shall not dwell on this town at present. From this point, I boarded the steamboat to go downstream as far as Ironton and it was a pleasure to view the scenery for the 40-mile trip. The Welsh people have played a very important part in the history of Ironton. Indeed, it can be said that they established and constructed the city. Although youngish, it is very orderly and it has a population of many thousands. The city's main officials, past and present, are Welshmen. They are very conspicuous as merchants but are mainly occupied in the ironworks and rolling-mills. Almost every mill is set up under the supervision of some Welshman, and regardless of many different nationalities making up the workforce, the main officials are invariably Welsh.

There used to be a Welsh Wesleyan church in Ironton but these days its services are conducted in English. That is the trend, I'm afraid. The Welsh are abandoning their language in this country and many of them frequent English churches. Indeed many English churches have Welshmen as deacons. The Congregational and Calvinistic Methodist churches in Ironton are still holding their services in Welsh, but no doubt these two will eventually give way to the English language. Of the three Welsh denominations in this part of America, it is the Baptist church that yields to English first of all; the Congregationalists come second and the Calvinistic Methodists last. I wonder if this is the pattern throughout the country. If so, what accounts for it?

From Ironton, I travelled to Portsmouth – another large town on the north side of the Ohio River. About 30 miles south of Ironton (not in Gallipolis, please note), Welsh immigrants disembark to go to the Welsh settlement of 'Jackson and Gallia'. Some of Portsmouth's residents work in the smelting-furnaces. There is a Welsh Methodist church here but the Cause is somewhat weak, although the chapel is a grand one. Reverend Siôn Edwards used to live here some time ago; also Reverend Edward Jones, formerly of Cincinnati. Mr Jones was a native of Blaenplwyf, near Aberystwyth, and was considered by many as a Father Figure of Methodism in the state of Ohio. The late Reverend J. Hughes, Liverpool, has written articles about this gentleman in the paper *Y Methodist* [The Methodist].

The Welsh community in the county of 'Jackson and Gallia' in southern Ohio is the oldest settlement in the state, and as far as our nation is concerned it is one of the main ones in the entire country. Cardiganshire has provided the majority of its inhabitants and many refer to it as the 'Cardiganshire of America'. In the year 1814, John Jones and his family from Tir Bach, near Cilcennin, were the first to arrive. They had intended to go to a place called Paddy's Run, but when they were in Gallipolis, their flatboat was damaged and it took several days to have it repaired. John and his family decided to use this spare time to go and visit a relative of theirs who lived near Granville – 150 miles north of where they had landed. After they went as far as northern Gallia, the settlers from England persuaded them to stay with them. They agreed, but endured much hardship because they lived in forest country and had to be self-sufficient. They dried Indian corn to make coffee and grew flax to provide themselves with linen for garments. Eventually, they progressed to own sheep and some of the wool was spun for clothing. At the beginning, the Indian corn had to be taken a long way to be ground. After a few years, a mill turned by two horses was used for this operation. The owner of the Indian corn had to make sure that he had horses to turn the mill and very often he would have to join a queue, which could mean a wait of several days: *Y cyntaf i'r felin a ga'i falu* [the first to the mill gets the flour – or, first come, first served].

---

[1] The newspaper *Y Wasg* (gwasg: press) was established in 1871 by a Welsh company in Pittsburgh, Pennsylvania.

[2] James W. Dale, *Inquiry into the Usage of Baptizo* (1869).

[3] *Twm o'r Nant*: bardic name of Thomas Edwards (1739–1810), Welsh-language dramatist and poet.

[4] Two Worlds: Earth and Heaven.

[5] Latter Day Saints: those of The Mormon Faith.

[6] Campbellites: members of the sect known as 'Disciples of Christ' founded by Alexander Campbell (1788–1866).

9

The Welsh People of Ohio

During the years 1834-40, huge immigration from Wales to Ohio took place. Many prominent persons like William Jones, Cofadail and Edward Morris, Llanddeiniol, were amongst the people who uprooted themselves from their country of birth and settled in this state. A church established in Moriah in 1835 by Reverend Edward Jones, Cincinnati. The minister appointed as foster-father and bishop of religious causes in this area was Reverend Robert Williams, who arrived from Wales in the autumn of 1836. Mr Williams passed away four years ago [1877], but is still mourned by people of this region. A minister who arrived in Ohio six months before Reverend Williams was Reverend Edward Blunt. He was a powerful preacher and accomplished excellent work for the Lord during difficult times. He prepared the way through many avenues and was a hard-working farmer as well as a minister of religion. He travelled far and wide, enduring the heat of summers and the extreme cold of winters; he plodded through forests, snow and mud to establish churches – all for hardly any acknowledgement except having his dream come true. His aspiration was accomplished beyond expectation.

There are now ten Methodist churches in this settlement – all quite close to each other. They are: Moriah, Horeb, Soar, Bethel, Sardis, Peniel, Centerville, Bethania, Jackson and Oak Hill; the latter has one of the most ornate chapels that the Welsh possess in this country. Ten ministers officiate within this circuit – similar to the system applied in Liverpool, England. The Congregationalists also have six chapels here: Oak Hill, Centerville, Nebo, Tynrhos, Carmel and Siloam, and these chapels are served by six preachers. The Baptists have four chapels with three ministers officiating: Oak Hill, Centerville, Bethlehem and Ebenezer.

The Welsh in this settlement are more old-fashioned in their approach to religion than people back home in Cardiganshire. This is not because of their lack of respect towards clergymen since I have not come across people anywhere who appreciate their ministers more. They are very capable and charitable, so it is not a lack of intelligence or generosity either. When one considers the population, no other place on earth has contributed as much as these people towards the distribution of Bibles amongst pagans. They donate approximately the same sum towards the Bible Society as they do towards their local ministry. Some of their views tend to be very old-fashioned but they strongly hold on to the virtues of godliness and family values; they are unassuming and peaceful folk. Oak Hill is supreme as far as chapels are concerned, and I hope other parts of the settlement will follow its example.

Agriculture is not a very good option in this area since the soil is poor and rugged and therefore not very fruitful. Iron is mined here, resulting in several blast-furnaces being set up. The best iron is melted to make wheels, railroad carriages and so forth. The Jefferson Furnace, near Oak Hill, is the largest one. It does not look impressive, situated underneath a bank, yet it has provided the Welsh owners with enough wealth to build mansions on the hilltops. The blast-furnaces have made many a Welshman very rich. The Welsh nation is in the majority in this region and many people have attained high positions with the Welsh 'ruling the roost' in commerce, politics and religion.

It is appropriate to mention the Honourable Thomas Ll. Hughes, a well-known man – not only in Ohio but also amongst all Welsh people throughout the country, especially the Methodists. Mr Hughes is a literary man and has written many articles for *Y Cyfaill*; his writing is educational and touches on religious history. His book *Yr Emmanuel* is ready for the press and will be published shortly by Reverend Thomas R. Jones. It will be a valuable contribution towards Welsh literature in America. Mr Hughes came to Oak Hill several years ago and became engaged in a small business, one in which others had failed to make a mark. His honesty and competence attracted the public and the business flourished. However, he was persuaded to join the Jefferson Furnace Company and was appointed as Secretary of the firm. After he served as Justice of the Peace for several years, he was selected to represent the county in the State Legislature in 1871. He is a man to be admired and emulated. He gets up at four in the morning and spends two hours reading the Bible in order to provide his soul with 'comforting thoughts'. He reads the Bible in Welsh and in English 'because the lights and shades present themselves more comprehensively by reading the scriptures in both languages'. That is his line of thinking anyway. Mr Hughes is like the lark; he wakes his family at six and after grace and breakfast, he sets off to his office. He has retired from his duties at Jefferson's now in order to concentrate on his own literary work. He is a native of Denbighshire and a friend of the late Morris Davies,[1] Bangor, with whom he corresponded right up to Davies' death. Mr Hughes is a faithful and much respected deacon.

Jackson is the capital of Jackson County. It is slightly outside the Welsh settlement but is getting Cymricised quite rapidly! A Welsh church, under the supervision of Reverend D. J. Jenkins, a cousin of Reverend Morris Morgan, has been established in Jackson and an eminent Welshman by the name of John J. C. Evans is Probate Judge in the city.

The district of Moriah is considered the mother and centre of the Welsh districts but the village of Oak Hill, 3 miles from Moriah, is foremost because the railroad from Portsmouth to Jackson runs through the parish. About 4 miles on the west side of Moriah, one finds several hamlets scattered randomly across the neighbourhood. The worst aspect of this settlement is its muddy roads. The roads in Wales are better maintained than the ones in America. The roads in 'Jackson and Gallia' are amongst the worst in the country and the main reason for this is the fact that large wagons are pulled along them to transport iron, pig iron, coke and so forth, to the furnaces. These wagons are pulled by four or five couples of oxen or crossbred mules. Between the rough countryside and the snow and ice melting on the craggy roads, rambling along made me fantasise that I was being very brave. However, a kind Samaritan noticed my predicament and I was provided with a strong horse to carry me, so all was well in the end. The residents of 'Jackson and Gallia' are very kind people and one would have to go very far to equal them. Ten years ago, I had the privilege of living in their midst for seven months.

[1] Morris Davies, Bangor (1796–1876), literary man, hymnologist and musician.

10

Cincinatti; Paddy's Run; Sugar Creek; Venedocia

From the town of Jackson, I had about 150 miles to travel to Cincinnati – the city which was considered years ago, and to some extent even today, as the Queen of the West. It is situated in the south-west of the state, on the banks of the Ohio River. The town of Covington, Kentucky, is parallel to it on the other side of the water. The first name given to Cincinnati was Losantville, when translated means 'the town opposite the outflow'. It was established in 1788 and was given its present name in 1790. Cincinnati is the largest city in the state of Ohio and records show that from 1800 to 1880 its population grew from 750 to 400,000. Among the inhabitants are Scots, Germans, French, Irish, English, and Welsh, as well as people from Asia and Africa. Cincinnati, at one time, had the largest abattoir for pigs in the world. Chicago has taken the lead on this score, the same as in other businesses. Cincinnati is a splendid city, and although it is enclosed by the river on one side and jagged rocks and hills on the other – each side appearing as if it was hostile to the other – this setting does not stop its development.

Reverend M. A. Ellis, the city's Methodist minister, met me at the railroad station and we proceeded to Lane's Theological School, where Mr Ellis and his family reside within the compound of the school. This School is renowned, especially amongst the Welsh. It was established in 1832 by Reverend Lyman Beecher, father of Reverend Henry Ward Beecher. It has six lecturers on its staff and the most senior is Reverend Llywelyn Ioan Evans. Next in rank is another Welshman, Reverend Morris, and another lecturer by the name of Humphreys also considers himself Welsh. Many young men from Wales have studied theology at this School.

There are three Welsh churches in Cincinnati – Calvinistic Methodist, Congregational and Baptist. There is another United Welsh Church in Covington with its members having backgrounds of different denominations. The minister of the Congregational chapel is Reverend D. Jones and the Methodist one is supervised by Reverend M. A. Ellis. Mr Ellis has announced that he hopes to visit Wales next summer. He is one of the main stalwarts of the Calvinistic Methodist Connection in America. He is sociable and a true gentleman in every sense of the word. He is also a brilliant scholar and a very powerful preacher, possessing good-humoured combinations of being a theologian, bard and philosopher. His sermons and compositions, although intellectual, are appealing to people in all walks of life. He is, undoubtedly, an influential figure in this region, not only in the pulpit but also in dealings with *eisteddfodau*, the press and other concerns. When he arrives in Wales, he is sure to have a warm welcome. If he is asked to give lectures on America whilst in his home country, I am sure he will do so with conviction. Almost every visiting preacher who comes to America is asked to give lectures on the trip upon his return to his native land, but however interesting these lectures may be, they are only recollections of travellers after all is said and done. Tourists do not really know what it is like to live on a daily basis in any country. However, I cannot think of anyone better acquainted with America than Mr Ellis, therefore I am sure that his lectures depict a true picture of life in this country.

The oldest Welsh settlement in the state of Ohio, Paddy's Run, lies approximately 20 miles north of Cincinnati. Here one finds agricultural land, making the circumstances of farmers from Wales very favourable. Welsh religious services were conducted in the Congregational chapel here for a long time but they have been anglicised by now, or rather Americanised! Over the years the Welsh, as well as other nationalities who have settled in this country, have gradually abandoned their native language. The Congregational chapel is under the ministerial guidance of Reverend J. L. Davies, son of the late Reverend Evan Davies, Tynrhos, Gallia County. Farmland in this area is worth between 50 and 100 dollars per acre and the landowners are happy with their livelihoods. However, they well remember that around forty years ago [early in the nineteenth century], when they arrived in America, they were very poor. The countryside was covered with trees then but clearance has taken place, resulting in areas which used to be forest-country becoming more costly than other farmland.

Gomer is a Welsh village in the middle of Paddy's Run, and a large, beautiful chapel has been erected there by the Congregationalists. Most chapels in America have decorative spires and this chapel is no exception. A spacious lecture-room is attached to the chapel and on special occasions, such as important festivals and quarterly meetings, the partition between the chapel and this extension is drawn back in order to have extra space. The chapel has 450 members but are without a minister at present. However, I understand that Reverend R. Mawddwy Jones from Wales has answered positively to the call of being their shepherd.

On my way to the settlement of Sugar Creek, about 7 miles north of Gomer, I stopped in the village of Vaughnsville.

Flat, fertile land is found here but not quite as rich as that found in Gomer. The elderly gentleman Jenkin Hughes (nephew of the late Reverend James Hughes, the interpreter from London, England), is the foster-father of this settlement. When he arrived in America, Mr Hughes declined the invitation to live amongst the Welsh in the settlement of 'Jackson and Gallia'. He told the people who had settled there: 'Since I have come all this distance from Wales to seek a better land, I have no desire to live in the hills again; therefore I shall venture farther to seek more fertile land.' To Putman he came, and today the wisdom of his judgement is evident. There are two small Welsh churches in Putman – one affiliated to the Methodists and another to the Congregationalists. Reverend John W. Morgans is the Methodist minister.

From this region, I travelled west through the town of Delphos, to the Welsh settlement of Venedocia, in Van Wert County – a distance of about 20 miles. This area also has excellent, flat land. I was very surprised to witness so many changes here since my last visit twelve years ago. Then, Salem stood on its own, in remote countryside and far from any railroad. Nowadays, this Methodist chapel is surrounded by elaborate farmhouses – more modish than any in Wales. It is large and comfortable, although quite plain inside. It has a membership of around 250. Horeb is another Methodist chapel, situated 2 miles from Salem but this chapel is quite ornate.

In another direction, 3 miles from Salem, a United Church has been founded. These three churches are under the ministry of Reverend John P. Morgan, who is highly esteemed by his congregations. Mr Morgan accompanied Reverend J. C. Davies of Pittsburgh on a visit to Wales last summer. The Methodists give their blessing to the

Congregationalists in Gomer and the Congregationalists reciprocate by agreeing to the Methodists holding on to Van Wert. The people in these settlements have come to a conclusion that it is wiser to have one strong congregation rather than splitting into small gatherings here and there.

11

Chicago; Wisconsin; Agriculture

After completing my mission in Ohio, I boarded the train for Chicago, Illinois. This meant I had to go through northern Indiana without stopping there this time. Very few Welsh people have settled in this region. After travelling 200 miles overnight, I arrived in the windy city of Chicago. It is the third most important city in America and is situated near Lake Michigan. It is comparatively young but is the focal point as far as transport and communication are concerned. In 1871, it experienced one of the worst disasters imaginable, when it was almost totally engulfed by fire; most of its magnificent buildings were destroyed but no time was wasted before it was rebuilt and apart from a few eyesores, it is grander than ever today.

Meat processing is the main industry in Chicago and the city has many abattoirs where meat is cut, salted and packed – on average one pig every 18 seconds. This city is also an important grain processing centre and has many railroads converging upon its centre, making the network comparable to a spider's web. Chicago is indeed a famous city, and like other large urban areas, it is impossible to elaborate about every activity that takes place there, that is, within the boundaries of a report such as this. Many Welsh people live in Chicago and many Welsh religious Causes have been established. The Methodist church is flourishing under the ministry of Reverend David Harries. He is very caring towards all of us Welsh people and this feeling is reciprocated by all who know him. Mr Harries' pastorate covers a wide area and he is very conscientious when dealing with his workload. He is also well thought of by both Welsh and American officials of different organisations. Not long ago, one gentleman presented Mr Harries with 500 dollars, so that his son could study theology at one of the best Institutes in the country. The boy had already turned down a place at a commercial college. I did not have a chance to meet the lad as he was away on holiday with his sponsor's son when I met his father.

When I was walking along with Reverend Harries one day, we met an English-speaking lady by the roadside. 'Good morning madam,' the minister said, whilst lifting his hat. Harries told me afterwards that this lady was very generous; that she was from England and belonged to a Presbyterian church.

He went on to say that he had once met her in a store and that she had said to him: 'It is a cold morning, Mr Harries, please accept 50 dollars to buy yourself an overcoat.' No doubt, you readers in Wales, remember Mr Harries when he was over with you. He has been to Wales twice and I would not be surprised if you see him again. He is a nephew of the late Reverend John Jones, Llanedi, Carmarthenshire. His health has not been too good of late but now that spring is here, he seems to be recovering.

From Chicago, I went 40 miles north to Racine, Wisconsin – another city on the banks of Lake Michigan. This city is situated on the railroad line between Chicago and Milwaukee and has a population of around 18,000. It was here the first Welsh immigrants to the area settled. There are two well-attended Welsh churches in this city, one by Calvinistic Methodists with the young and energetic Reverend John Roberts as minister; the other church is affiliated to the Congregationalists under the ministry of Reverend John P. Williams, who is another talented and honourable young man. Racine is famous for its *eisteddfodau,* more so than anywhere else in the country, I believe. Many Welsh people have lived in Racine and some have made a name for themselves in religion, politics and the military. The Honourable W. W. Vaughan and Reverend Ll. T. Evans D. D. are two I can name but there are many more.

I had another 20 miles to travel before reaching Milwaukee, the largest city in Wisconsin. Milwaukee has a smart, clean appearance with splendid buildings, wide roads and a welcoming atmosphere. Like Racine, it is situated on the west side of Lake Michigan. There are many Welsh religious Causes in Milwaukee. The Methodist minister is Reverend H. P. Howells; he draws a large crowd to his beautiful, capacious chapel. The stained-glass windows alone have cost 1,000 dollars. The pulpit and pews are carved from the best mahogany and are covered with multi-coloured, velvet cushions for the congregation's comfort. Mr Howells, himself, complements this adornment since he is handsome and a gentleman in every sense of the word. He could be on a par with any aristocrat in Wales because he has a majestic personality, and enough admirers who would precede him shouting 'ABREC',[1] if that was the custom of the country. However, Mr Howells does not succumb to pomp and adulation.

Congregationalist and Baptist members of this district must forgive me for dwelling on the Methodists. In a previous letter, I mentioned that the Methodists were lagging behind in the industrial areas of Pennsylvania and eastern Ohio but in Wisconsin they are in the majority. There are many admirable Welshmen in Milwaukee. John Jones from Pontrhydfendigaid is a deacon and his son holds a high position within the railroad network. Another young man, Gwilym Eryri,[2] a native of Beddgelert, north Wales, has been appointed as an assistant to the Welsh regarding connections to the railroads.

Gwilym Eryri

I have been told that a young Welsh lady is paid an annual sum of 1,000 dollars to sing in one of the city's church choirs and another young lady receiving 1,500 dollars to sing a different voice in the same choir. Every choir member receives a payment and many churches in the major cities follow the same reward practice. When I was in Wales, I heard grumblings amongst people that the annual salary of twenty pounds paid to their minister was exorbitant, whilst at the same time admitting that they were lucky to have one of the best clergymen in their county!

I believe that, as yet, there are more Welsh agricultural workers in Wisconsin than in any other state of the Union. The Waukesha settlement, about 25 miles west of Milwaukee, is the oldest agricultural one. I notice that land here, on the whole, is more level than in the eastern states. The countryside between Chicago and Milwaukee presents a very favourable view but Waukesha, the spot chosen by the Welsh, is rather hilly and rocky. It is said that the entire county of Waukesha was under water at one time; shells, reminders of that era, are still in the ground. The Welsh started settling here in the year 1840; most of them were from the counties of Anglesey and Cardiganshire. They would buy land from the government for 1¼ dollars per acre; others would purchase it second-hand for between 2½ to 10 dollars per acre. These days, land varies in its value from 20 to 60 dollars according to its condition and suitability. The Welsh farmers of this region are comfortable and quite independent. Only a few pay rent, and those who do intend doing so for just two or three years, since their aim is to own their farms. The tendency to go further west these days is causing the price of agricultural land to fall in this region. There are two railroads running through the centre of this settlement.

The wages of senior farm servants range from 20 to 25 dollars per month, and under-servants earn a monthly sum of around 18 dollars. They are paid for only eight months of the year. For the other four months, they can choose to have a rest and not work at all, or alternatively, take up odd jobs such as chopping firewood, which is paid so much per cord.[3] Some split rails; others shell Indian corn, which is paid so much per bushel. By doing such jobs, between 1 and 1¼ dollars per day can be earned. Many young farmhands prefer to live in farmhouses over the winter; they feed the animals each morning and evening for their keep and attend school during the day. A labourer's earnings are rated at about a dollar per day plus sustenance. During the wheat harvest, at the end of June and beginning of July, they can earn 2 to 2½ dollars per day. Again, during haymaking time, they can earn about 1½ dollars daily.

---

[1] An ancient Middle Eastern term meaning 'to pay obeisance to'. It occurs in Genesis 41:43: 'Pharoah ... had him ride in his second best chariot; and they cried before him, "Bow down ..."' (Complete Jewish Bible, 1998).

[2] Gwilym Eryri: W. E. Powell (1841–1910).

[3] Per cord: a term for a bundle fastened by cord.

12

Occupations; Waukesha County; the Civil War; Welsh Communities in Wisconsin

Women do not work on the land in this country and the rate for them when working in farmhouses is between 2 and 3 dollars per week. The trouble is, they are hard to come by since they prefer to go to the cities to work, where they can earn more. It is possible for women to be engaged in a variety of occupations which are performed indoors. They can be secretaries, lawyers, doctors, printers, engravers and suchlike, resulting in a shortage of waitressing positions in this country. Tailoring is another worthwhile occupation for women here. I heard a professional tailor, a member of the Academy of Tailors, mention that not many boys enter the profession in America and those who have qualified in the craft before entering the country have to be retrained in order to reach the expected American standard. A specified requirement also applies to other trades. Many immigrants find the situation perplexing when they arrive here; they soon lose patience with the system and decide to return to their homeland. They are not willing to get accustomed to American regulations and consider them to be superficial – aiming at the easy and fast methods in craftsmanship, rather than observing details such as plane specifications and so forth. The American, on the other hand, mocks natives of other countries on their method of using rod, plum-bob, tape and such devices. The Americans do not believe in sticking to elementary aspects of any trade. In their view, those should be second nature to any skilled worker so that assignments and deadlines can be achieved like the spread of an eagle's wing, without adhering to minute details. However, tradespeople who have come to this country and persevered for five years, by combining the American methods with what they have been trained in their homelands, turn out better workmanship than anyone.

To return to agricultural land in Waukesha: it is mostly fertile and very desirable, although some sections are hilly and rocky. Here and there, one sees beautiful lakes, especially towards Bark River, Ixonia and Watertown. Rows of tall poplars screen the roads and the ground has been covered with bushes. The layout of trees, bushes and lakes makes the whole area appear very scenic indeed. Farmhouses and buildings dot the landscape and the windmills are quite distinctive; it is impossible to miss their long ropes and planks. These windmills are used to draw clean water from the ground from a depth of between 20 to 50 feet but 30 feet is the usual measure. The water is used by the inhabitants for various purposes.

Religious affairs are top priority amongst the Welsh in Waukesha County. Those of you in Wales, who consider yourselves privileged, do not discount your kith and kin in the far west. They have persevered to keep the traditions of the patriarchs alive. Their priority has been to build a place of worship wherever they found themselves. Apart from the one in Racine, Jerusalem is the oldest Welsh church in the state of Wisconsin. It was in Jerusalem that the first *Cyfarfod Dosbarth*[1] and *Gymanfa*[2] were held.

At first, the services were held in dwellings such as Bronberllan, Gilfach-y-dwnfawr and Nant-y-calch. On one occasion, when the Honourable John H. Evans, the guardian of Methodism in the area, was preaching in Gilfach-y-dwnfawr, several half-naked Red Indians with feathers in their hair entered the house begging for bread and meat. After Mrs Evans, the lady of the house, went to the cellar to fetch food for them, they left peacefully and the service was not interrupted afterwards. After a while, a chapel made of wood was erected and it was named 'The Log Chapel'. Even before a roof was constructed, the people worshipped within its walls for one season. The pulpit was an old goods-box given by a shopkeeper and the pews and floorboards were made from planks cut from crossbeams. They travelled from afar to worship in this chapel, in whatever attire they happened to be wearing on the day. Being fashionable was not important to them.

Today's chapel, Jerusalem, is a grand building and has a large membership; it and Bethesda, another small but beautiful chapel, are supervised by Reverend Rowland H. Evans. Mr Evans is a very conscientious minister whose dedication to duty is evident in the community. The Welsh churches of Moriah, Soar and Seion have Reverend John Moses as their minister. He is a learned man, a powerful preacher and of a very generous nature. Both preachers, Evans and Moses, hope to travel to Wales within the next two years. I did not have the opportunity to call on Reverend John P. Williams this time. The chapel of Bethania, under the ministry of Reverend Hugh Roberts, is also in this region of Wisconsin. The Congregational chapel here has Reverend Cadwaladr D. Jones as minister. He is an authority on the plight and prowess of Welsh Americans and is quite willing to pass on the information he has collected. In Bark River, there are four Welsh churches. It would be better for chapels with only a few members to merge rather than carry on as separate units but the denomination factor is very strong amongst some people.

Young lads who were members of Methodist churches in this region of Wisconsin joined the army during the Great

Rebellion[3] and their camp was in Milwaukee. Orders were given for them to go to the battlefield in the South but before doing so, they were allowed to go home for a weekend to say farewell to their loved ones. They went to a Fellowship Meeting that Sunday and asked their fellow church members to pray for them. They left for the South on Monday.

The following week, a prayer meeting was held in one of Bark River's chapels, starting at 10 in the morning. The deacons remembered the requests of the soldiers but an account of one particular prayer, by a Welshman from Anglesey, has not been forgotten. This man was so earnest, in his plea to God to safeguard the boys, that tears were rolling down his cheeks and he addressed his Saviour thus: 'If our lads are on the front-line today, please God let your wings shield them. Please safeguard them from danger. Only you can make the enemy retreat so that our boys will be out of the perils associated with the conflict.'

In three days time, the *Sentinel* newspaper arrived with reports that the regiment the boys belonged to had been in the firing line between 10 and 11 on that particular Sunday morning, at the precise time the prayers were being delivered. The enemy had started to attack but for some unexplained reason, they decided on a ceasefire and pulled back. No doubt, the enemy would have been victorious if it had continued to advance but Bark River's deacons prayed for their boys. God listened to the prayers and instantly intervened. 'The effectual fervent prayer of a righteous man availeth much' (James 5:16).

Ixonia and Watertown are outside the boundary of Waukesha County. The village of Ixonia has a railroad station and two comfortable chapels – Congregational and Methodist. Watertown, on the other hand, is a fairly large town but it does not contain many Welsh residents. The

Methodists have one small church in the town and *Rachel o Fôn* [Rachel from Anglesey], the amusing lady preacher, is a member there. Family responsibilities prohibit her from ministerial duties nowadays but her heart is still glued to the vocation. She is planning on going to Wales in the near future. Gwyn, a bard from Swyddffynnon, Cardiganshire, also lives in Watertown. His son, editor of the paper *Watertown Democrat* was critically ill when I was in the locality. I do hope he is better by now.

The county of Iowa (not the state, please note) is at the southern point of the state of Wisconsin. To go there from Watertown, I had to go through Madison, the capital of the county. This small, urban district is clean and prosperous and the state house, situated at its centre, is very grand. I was tricked by my map when working out my route from Madison to Mineral Point because it showed, as one already in use, a railroad that had not been completed; therefore I had to figure out my journey over different lines for two complete days before reaching my destination at 9 o'clock one evening. My good friend, Robert Hughes, was patiently waiting for me at Mineral Point's railroad station. I had a few preaching appointments in this area and stayed at Reverend William Morris' home. Mr Morris is a nephew of the late William Morris, Cilgerran, west Wales.

The late Reverend John Davies, a man who is still fondly remembered in this state, used to be in charge of the Methodist chapel in the Picatonica[4] settlement. People remember Mr Davies as a very godly and influential person who was also a forceful preacher. His biography has been written by Reverend William Hughes.[5] This grand chapel in Picatonica draws a large congregation and the main officials are relatives of Reverend Davies. The Davies family originated from Pembrokeshire and were described as unconventional. I suppose it was a fitting description, since all six or seven siblings lived together in the same household well into old age, and although Reverend Davies was the youngest, he was deemed head of the family.

There are other Welsh chapels, by other denominations, in the Picatonica settlement.

The land is hilly and rocky in this part of the country and therefore not suitable for agricultural purposes. Three kinds of peat are dug from the bogs of this region; they are lead, dry bones and black jack. Zinc is produced from black jack, which is a sort that resembles coal.

After fulfilling my appointments, I returned to Mineral Point and the following morning, Robert Hughes took me in his buggy 8 miles northwards to Dodgeville. According to my schedule, I was supposed to conduct the service at a chapel there at 10 in the morning. After arriving at my point of call, I discovered that there had been a change of plan and that I was expected to preach in Salem, which was 4 miles farther. Reverend William Charles harnessed his fast mare to his buggy and we galloped for most of the journey and reached Salem almost on time. Reverend John H. Evans, one of the first Welsh ministers to settle in this district, lives near Salem. He is elderly now, yet cheerful and sociable. Another Welshman, Reverend Griffith Jones, also lives in the area.

I was back in Dodgeville that Sunday by six in the evening, preaching to an interdenominational congregation – Methodists, Congregationalists and Baptists. The Methodist minister at Dodgeville is Reverend William Charles, Gwalchmai, Anglesey. Mrs Charles is the daughter of the famous bard, *Eos Glan Twrch*.[6] The Congregationalist minister here is Reverend Sam Phillips, a good-natured man whose kindness and guidance radiates amongst people in all walks of life. Mr Phillips is a bachelor and middle-aged by now. The Baptist pastor is Reverend Meredith Evans. I did not have much opportunity to socialise with Mr Evans because he lived in the country and some distance from my stopping places. I have heard that he is a very generous man and well-liked in his neighbourhood.

From Dodgeville, Reverend Charles transported me in his buggy for 18 miles to Prairie Chapel by Blue Mound which is the highest point between the Alleghenies and the Rockies. Bethel, another chapel, is situated 6 miles north of Prairie Chapel. Both chapels are equidistant from Blue Mound. The number of Welsh people in this area has diminished but I did meet Reverend John H. Davies, formerly of Pantcoch, west Wales. He had been over to his homeland 8 years previously and had given lectures on 'America' in several places. He was not a minister of religion at that time, though. He wishes to be remembered to the people who were kind to him when his wife was treated by Dr Thomas at a Liverpool hospital. She is now free from the pain she suffered in her foot after unsuccessful attempts by fourteen American doctors to cure her.

I came across a strange Welsh character, someone I shall not name, in this area. He had been married for some time. However, when he was away from home once, he became acquainted with another girl and came to the conclusion that this girl would make him a better wife than the one he already had. He told his girlfriend that he was a bachelor and married her. This predicament landed him in big trouble because his lawful wife instructed officials to start legal proceedings against him. He decided to make himself scarce and lived rough in caves and other shelters. He would often knock on people's doors, and was sometimes allowed to enter, but he always wanted to know where the door to the cellar was in all houses. He would also ask the occupiers to let him know if they saw strangers approaching their premises. Whenever he heard dogs barking or a knock on a door, he would jump and creep down to the cellar. Sometimes, mischievous children, who knew that this man was inside certain houses, would knock on doors just to scare him!

The outcome of this saga was that his legal wife agreed to a divorce; he then had to marry his girlfriend, officially, to obliterate the bigamy he had committed. At first, the girl did not see why she had to marry the second time since there had been no deceit on her part. To conform to legal requirements, they did have another wedding ceremony; unfortunately, they were again not within the law, because a letter confirming the divorce had not been presented. This letter was soon produced since the first wife had no objection by this time. A third wedding was arranged and the marriage was validated this time. *Rhaff dair cainc ni thorrir ar frys* [A three-strand rope is not broken in haste]: I would think that this proverb is applicable here.

This man was not law-abiding in other ways, really. On one occasion, when he was unsure of his whereabouts and was being sought by the men of law, he stopped at an inn, and after disclosing his predicament to the innkeeper, he asked for directions to his home. The innkeeper told him to go a certain way and that he would try and catch up with him a little later. This gave the innkeeper time to tell his daughter to go after the man immediately, in order to tell him to hasten and hide in a certain spot. The police arrived at the inn and the innkeeper accompanied them to the forest on a different route but 'the bird' had escaped and was nowhere to be seen!

This man told me that he had tried out several religious denominations which the Welsh practised in America. He had been a Methodist, Congregationalist, Wesleyan and a

Baptist. Indeed, he had explored all avenues but had failed to find the road to heaven amongst any of them. However, he did tell me that, at last, he had found the 'route' and that he had no doubts whatsoever this time. He could see heaven as clear as the sun in the sky on a bright day. He had discovered 'the way' with people who did not believe that hell existed. To be serious about the matter, he could not have found a better faith than one which protects sinners from hell!

---

[1] *Cyfarfod Dosbarth*: meeting of Ministers and Laymen.

[2] *Cymanfa*: General Assembly of Methodist Churches.

[3] 'The Great Rebellion': The American Civil War, 1860–65.

[4] This place-name in Wisconsin is spelt Pecatonica today.

[5] *Cofiant Y John Davies* (Memoirs of John Davies) – Picatonica, Wisconsin (1878).

[6] *Eos Glan Twrch*: John Edwards (1806–1887), poet and prose writer.

13

Improvements in Travel; Settlers' Lives; Welsh Prairie; Proscairon

It was more difficult to come to America years ago [the end of the eighteenth and beginning of the nineteenth centuries] than it is these days. It used to take six weeks to cross the Atlantic, whereas the voyage now takes only ten days. It used to take two weeks to travel from New York to Wisconsin, but this journey can now be accomplished in two days. Years ago, clumsy carriages pulled by horses, often in canals, were used as means of going from one place to another. This system was followed by rough wagons which were covered with canvas that swayed in the wind whilst people travelled through forests and wilderness to find a spot where they could settle. These travellers would spend days in their wagons; they were their sleeping quarters as well as their abode during daylight hours. Flies were often a nuisance, especially at night.

In contrast, today one can sit on comfortable seats in trains that speed ahead to different destinations. A long time ago, immigrants to this country had to live their entire lives without conveniences such as railroads and market-places. The railroads penetrate many areas now and farmers use the freight-trains to transport their produce to retailers in different urban areas. Much ground was levelled out in order to construct railroad tracks and stations. Our forefathers ventured and faced many perils but their descendants are reaping their fruits. Why are people so complacent in Wales, I wonder? Why do they suffer oppression under wealthy landowners rather than board ship to a free country such as America, when the process of emigration has become so straightforward?

The people of Wisconsin, just as people in other states, like to narrate tales about their ancestors' beginnings in this country. John O. Owens, Proscairon,[1] a native of Llanddeiniolen, Caernarfonshire, recollects that four trees were the corner-poles of his first house. Boards were nailed to tree-trunks to create rear, front and side. The other side was made of earth and turfs and the fireplace and chimney were placed on this side.

Snakes would lurk under floorboards and other surfaces in houses such as Mr Owens'.

'Go and call your father and tell him that lunch is ready,' Mrs Owens said to her daughter one day. Away the girl went, barefoot, as is customary with children during summertime in this country.

She had gone only a few yards before she returned to the house shouting, 'Mam, Mam!'

'Whatever is the matter?' Mrs Owens asked.

'There are snakes everywhere,' the girl replied. Mrs Owens grabbed a big stick and could not believe her eyes when she saw the assemblage of interweaving snakes so close to the house. She started to clobber them with her stick but in no time, Mr Owens arrived on the scene to help. As many as thirty-eight of the reptiles were killed that day, but the number that escaped was much higher. One does not come across snakes in such quantity these days.

Years ago, when a new family arrived in a settlement, the neighbours would turn up on a specific day to help with the construction of a house. The sides and floors were made of planks of wood measuring around 20 feet in length and a 'tongue and groove' method was usually adopted. The wall joints were dabbed with mortar. A door, two windows, a fireplace and a chimney were added and the roof was made of clapboards. This gathering of helpful neighbours in house construction was called the 'rising bee'.[2] During that era, a group of friends would sanction a 'bee' on other occasions, such as with maize harvesting. This particular task was called the 'busking bee' which was a process of detaching husks or leaves from the spikes of the Indian corn. This is a procedure used when harvesting maize whereas threshing is the custom with other cereal plants. Again, if a mother found that she was short of warm clothing for her family at wintertime, the neighbours would arrange a 'sewing bee' or a 'quilting bee' and one can be sure that such an event would be a first rate 'talking bee'! Help with chopping wood was called a 'chopping bee', and a 'hauling bee' when transporting timber. The custom has caught on in Wales and 'spelling bees' take place there.

The ploughing of virgin land was the paramount task for first-time settlers. Up to seven pairs of oxen would pull a plough with one man holding the plough's handles, another man driving the animals and another walking ahead, pulling up weeds and roots before the plough came into contact with them. I was told by the people of Columbus, Ohio, that oxen were the animals used for all work by the first settlers in America. The Honourable Hugh Jones was the first in the Columbus area to own a horse – a bay mare with speckled eyes. She is remembered by everyone who saw her since it was unusual to see a horse in this country years ago.

Sledge-cars were the first vehicles used by settlers,

followed by wagon-trucks which were made entirely of wood – wheels and all. These trucks were used to carry wood, farm produce and also to convey people to their places of religious worship. One American gave a lecture mocking the Welsh for their method of travelling in these trucks, especially on Sundays. It was the noise that bothered Americans mostly, because the entire neighbourhood would know when the Welsh were passing through. The oxen would bellow at the crack of the whips, and the wooden wheels would squeak. People came from south, east and west and would pass right in front of houses occupied by Americans. However, in the book *History Of Columbia* County, published recently,[3] the American author endeavours to promote better Christian understanding of the Welsh people's way of life. This man endorses their religious zealousness. Today, nobody is perturbed by the sound of church bells on Sundays. Many people stay in their beds all morning!

My next port of call in Franklin County was Columbus. One could say that it is a town; it is definitely a large village and has a railroad running through it. There is one Welsh church affiliated to the Calvinistic Methodists here, and Uriah Davies, a distinguished man in state affairs, is a deacon and represents this church on the Methodist Connection[4]. There are three other churches in the surrounding countryside namely Moriah, Salem and Bethel, the latter being the mother-church. Reverend John J. Roberts is bishop of these churches. I had heard of him before and by the way he was described, I envisaged a person big in stature and, maybe, an authoritarian. Not so, indeed. Mr Roberts is fairly short and a no-nonsense person. If I did not know otherwise, I would not have thought that he held an important position. People within his diocese regard him as *mwyaf o holl feibion y gorllewin* [the most influential man in the west]. That remark is something to be reckoned with, when it comes from people he has been officiating over for thirty-five years.

The settlement of Welsh Prairie was my next stop. Jerusalem has the smallest chapel-building in this region. Nevertheless, of all the chapels in the community, it has the highest number of members. Mr J. R. Jones, *Bardd yr Hendre* [Hendre's bard] is a member in Jerusalem and will be ordained minister this coming summer. Another chapel is Seion, which is the earliest of all the churches, and going by the picture of it in my programme, it does have an antiquated appearance. Carmel, another chapel, is the spiritual home of the Honourable William J. Jones, one of the three brother preachers from Llanllyfni.[5] He is approaching eighty but in high spirits and his sermons are always uplifting and interesting. We last met nine years ago on the *City of Baltimore*, when we were both returning to Wales.

I do know that the first Welsh religious services held in America were in Log Cabins and during summertime; people would go to the woods and sit on the thickest tree-stumps to hold their *seiadau* [fellowship meetings]. The Welsh made good use of these meetings to reminisce about their upbringing in Wales and their experiences after arriving in America, especially the establishment of the Christian faith and its progression in these parts. Long ago, monthly religious meetings were held in cowsheds and calf-pens where ceilings were so low that people had to crouch throughout the services. It was a 'bring your own stool' practice in these outbuildings and the stools were usually blocks of wood. Sometimes, planks were placed on wooden stumps to create benches. Needless to say, conditions were not ideal and if someone was not used to farm odours, the experience was not very pleasant! William Jones did tell me that these were memorable meetings; people did feel the presence of God and there was always a friendly atmosphere amongst the attendees.

In the early days, the Welsh in America felt *hiraeth* for their relatives and surroundings back in Wales, yet this longing brought them closer to each other and made them count their blessings. After all, they were in a free country and prospects were good. They felt that fair play was more evident in America, although life was tough at the beginning. They applied their newfound freedom to worshipping God, their Lord and Creator, and when they attended religious services, they felt that the Lord had provided their souls with tranquillity and peace of mind. They did not have many possessions; their furniture was plain and their crockery unadorned, yet they were content.

Several worthy deacons came from Wales to this district many years ago. Ten were members of Seion Chapel. Reverend Hugh Jones, Columbus, made the following remark: 'The Lord has not given us many Welsh preachers but he has made sure that a good number of able deacons have come over from the homeland.'

My next destination was Randolph, a charming village in delightful surroundings. There are two very decorative chapels here – Methodist and Congregational. Reverend Thomas R. Jones lives in Randolph. I am acquainted with two other Welshmen who live here, namely Thomas Foulkes who is referred to as *eich Ewythr o'r Cwm* [your Uncle from the Valley] and John Roberts, Announcements Organiser for the General Assembly of the Methodist church.

Six miles further west is the village of Cambria, the centre of Welsh settlements in this part of America. It is not quite as flourishing as Randolph but law and order prevails and I was dutiful to accomplish Matthew 10.11 in this community: 'And into whatsoever city or town ye shall enter, enquire who in it is worthy; and there abide till ye go thence'. Reverend Rees Evans, a Calvinistic Methodist minister, lives in Cambria and there are several Welsh churches in the locality.

My next stop was Portage Prairie, another Welsh settlement where people are very conscious of their religion. A very impressive chapel with a high steeple has been erected in the countryside but it would not look out of place in the centre of any city. The Methodists have a mobile ministry in this area, the same as in Wales. The minister would be the one who happened to live in the neighbourhood, regardless of the denomination he belonged to.

I continued my journey to Rock Hill, a place situated at the corner of the settlement where land is uneven. Reverend David Pugh has worked diligently in Rock Hill for many years. He is not under contract to any chapel nor is there an agreed sum of money paid for his devotion. It is evident that he is in charge, though, and he and his family lead comfortable lifestyles. In contrast, some people seek publicity like 'jack o'lanterns'[6] but often meet up with disappointments in the end.

From Rock Hill, I travelled to Proscairon where the late Reverend Thomas H. Roberts lived. My next stop was Blaen-y-Cae [top of the field], or Engedi,[7] as it is known by some, where the oldest church in this part of the settlement is found. The chapels in Proscairon and Lake Emily are branches of this church, in the same way as

Jerusalem, Carmel and Cambria are subdivisions of Seion at the other end of the community. The religious Cause is maintained in Engedi and the surrounding area by Reverend John R. Daniel. He is a slight man and appears to be nervous when meeting people he is not familiar with. However, I am told that he is a powerful preacher, and has a great deal of influence over his flock, by all accounts.

I concluded my stay in this district by visiting Lake Emily. Welsh people from Anglesey and Caernarfonshire occupy a vast area here. They are fortunate to be living in a delightful district and they seem to be very happy. The countryside is a high, rolling prairie and the land has produced splendid crops of wheat for many years. Unfortunately, the last three or four years have proved a failure. Apparently, the chintz insects[8] caused damage to the crops but I am told that the cold, stormy weather we experienced earlier this year has killed these bugs, so hopefully all will be well this coming summer. Maize is grown in abundance in this district; there is also a tendency towards grazing, haying and animal husbandry. Although there is excellent land in this part of the country, the trend to move west is quite strong – especially to Dakota.[9] It is a blessing that the world is round!

From Emily, I had to go to the Welsh settlement of Oshkosh. Whilst waiting the arrival of a train at Fox Lake Station, I met a grey-haired, elderly man.

'Are you going far on this line?' the man enquired. 'Forgive me for being inquisitive. I am fond of company and enjoy talking to people,' he continued.

Myself: I am quite happy for you to do the talking; I shall enjoy listening. By the way, I am going to Oshkosh.

Fellow: Do you live in Oshkosh?

Evans: No, sir, I live on the other side of the Atlantic.

Fellow: Really, whereabouts then?

Evans: In Wales.

Fellow: Well, well. Where in Wales? I have been to Europe and stayed in north Wales many years ago. I am acquainted with other regions of Wales, mind you. From what part of Wales do you come?

Evans: From Cardiganshire – the Aberystwyth area.

Fellow: How long have you been over here?

Evans: About six months

Fellow: For how long do you intend to stay?

Evans: I shall stay for another six months.

Fellow: Which areas in America have you been to?

Evans: As yet, I have visited several Welsh settlements and Vermont.

Fellow: What is your mission? Is it just a pleasure trip?

Evans: No, I hope to write a book about the Welsh in America.

Fellow: What perceptions do you have of America and the lifestyles of the Welsh settlers?

Evans: Well, I have to say the same as they themselves conclude: that this is a very good country and sailing to America was the best decision they ever made.

Fellow: I expect you want to go west, in order to find out about situations over there.

Evans: Yes, I intend to take a close look at all aspects.

Fellow: I thought that you probably had a certain purpose. I have a high regard for the Welsh. On the whole, they are very good citizens. If I can be of assistance to you at any time, please get in touch. I am known as William Davies, Fox Lake. Most people know me in this area.

Mr Davies happened to know another gentleman on the station's platform – the editor of the newspaper *Fox Lake Representative*. I was introduced to this gentleman and Mr Davies very kindly made this request of him on my behalf: 'Please mention this young man in the next issue of your paper and disclose that it was I who put his name forward and acclaimed his work.'

I gained valuable advice and instructions by this chance meeting with Mr Davies. He gave me names of some of his relatives who happened to be lawyers and bankers in the western states. He made it known to me that he had spent many years campaigning against slavery in America. He was born and brought up in Boston, so was a true Yankee! He had a good name in the Oberlin area and was a close friend of Reverend Charles G. Finney.[10] I told him that I had been a student at The Institute in Oberlin and had listened to several of Finney's sermons. Mr Davies and I discovered that we had a great deal in common and I later found out that he was a well-known lawyer.

I arrived in Oshkosh, a city situated on the banks of Lake Winnebago. This lake, 35 miles in length and half that measure in width, is too small to be included on the customary maps of the area. Until recently, Oshkosh was the second largest city in the state of Wisconsin. Racine has currently surpassed it as far as population is concerned. The countryside in this district is amongst the most spectacular I have set eyes on. It was in Gomer, Ohio, I witnessed the finest farm buildings. Nevertheless, both Gomer and Oshkosh districts have very good, fertile land although it is rather level and unvarying in Gomer, whereas the hills around Oshkosh complement the green valleys. Distribution of land is also very orderly in Oshkosh and the farms' outbuildings compare favourably with the ones in Gomer. All in all, the farmers in both districts are very happy with their circumstances. If I was paying rent for a 100-acre farm in Wales, I would have no hesitation in deciding what to do. I would pack my bag and sail over to America to buy my own holding.

The Calvinistic Methodists have two chapels in the Oshkosh area and are within 1½ miles of each other. Bethesda was the first erected and it has a manse attached to it, but it does not have a minister at present. Peniel is the other, with Reverend John K. Roberts ministering it. Reverend Parry is pastor of the Congregational chapel here and the Baptist chapel is under the ministerial guidance of Reverend H. C. Parry (*Cefni*)[11] – a well-known preacher and author. He was very ill with shingles when I was in his territory and therefore I did not have the pleasure of meeting him. However, I was given some of his work by his relative, Thomas Thomas, whose contribution to religious Causes has been invaluable. Reverend Humphrey R. Jones is minister of Bethel, the small Wesleyan chapel in the area. I shall have more to say about him in my next letter.

Recently, an amusing young man, affiliated to the Wesleyans, visited Welsh churches in Illinois and other states. Griffiths is his surname and he hails from north Wales. I understand that he has accepted an invitation to be minister of the Welsh Wesleyan Church in Utica, New York State. The ministry of Reverend E. Edmunds, in this region, has 'gone down like hot cakes', as the Americans would say! I believe that Reverend Thomas Thomas will also have a good following when he comes over from Wales this coming summer. The Welsh are always very emotional, wherever they may be. They delight in religious fervour and appreciate talent and rhetoric from their preachers.

The Welsh are quite numerous in Oshkosh with some of them holding high positions as merchants. The Methodists worship in a large, plain chapel. It is said that their young minister, Reverend David Davies, is one of the most promising in the state of Wisconsin. In contrast to the Methodists' chapel, the Congregationalists have a decorative building. It is not as spacious as some but it does have a tall, impressive spire. The Congregationalists do not have a minister at present.

Twelve miles north of Oshkosh, the town of Neenah is located; both urban areas are situated on the banks of Lake Winnebago. There are several Welsh people in this town and two small chapels – Congregational and Calvinistic Methodist. I was ahead of schedule when I arrived in Neenah, and had the pleasure to be present at one of the Methodists' weekly meetings. The Methodists only have nine members. Six were present, so it was well attended since two of the absentees were elderly. I was invited to start the service; then everyone participated and the atmosphere was captivating. 'Fear not, little flock; for it is your Father's good pleasure to give you the kingdom' (Luke 12:32). It was obvious to me that these people, although bereft of a minister, held on to high principles and were sincere in their worship.

The following evening I was preaching in the same chapel, but to a slightly larger congregation, because members of the other chapel had joined us. Since I had made a return journey to Milwaukee that day, it was assumed that I was tired, therefore one of the gentlemen officiated the preliminary parts for me. A father and daughter led the hymn-singing with everyone else joining in. This is how you find these small congregations – always at their best. Both Congregationalists and Methodists unite in all activities, except in *Y Seiat* [fellowship meeting]. The heavenly manna is amazing!

Large congregations in ornate chapels are no more privileged than the few who attend small, plain chapels. Unfortunately, one does find in some of the larger chapels that it is the minister, the deacons and a few other officials who preside, whilst the rest sit and listen. It is always good to see members contributing to services.

---

[1] *Early History of the Welsh in the Proscairon District of Wisconsin, The Source of the Name and Other Interesting Reminiscences*, Daniel Jenkins Williams. (Great Plains Welsh Heritage Project, January 2007).

[2] The use of the word 'bee' is common in literature describing colonial North America, and is an allusion to the social behaviour of the insect. The earliest known printed example of the term was the use of 'spinning bee' in 1769.

[3] *History of Columbia County*, by C. W. Butterfield. (Western History Publishing Company, Chicago, 1880).

[4] The Methodist Connection: group of churches forming a circuit of a quarterly meeting.

[5] Llanllyfni's three preachers, Richard, Hugh and William Jones. Llanllyfni is a village in north-western Wales.

[6] Jack o'Lantern (Will o' the Wisp): a mysterious light that was said to lead travellers from well-trodden paths into treacherous marshes.

[7] The name 'Engedi' derives from the small oasis which hid David from King Saul during the years he evaded Saul in the wilderness. In the USA today, 'Engedi' is a collective name for a group of churches affiliated to the Wesleyans.

[8] Striped or spotted chintz are a strain of insect that destroys grain.

[9] Dakota: the state of Dakota was not divided into North and South until 1889.

[10] Charles Grandison Finney (1792–1875): American Presbyterian minister, evangelist, revivalist and author.

[11] *Cefni*: pseudonym of Hugh Parry (1826–1895), Baptist minister, poet, litterateur and theologian.

14

Reverend H. R. Jones' Story

Since the amazing revival of 1857, I have been very keen to learn about the two Welsh apostles, Reverends H. R. Jones and D. Morgans. Nine years have passed since I saw Morgans and now I have the opportunity to meet up with Jones. Thinking about the two preachers brings Cowper's[1] words to mind:

God moves in a mysterious way
His wonders to perform.

Thomas D. Parry, formerly of Ysbyty Ystwyth, came to Bethesda to meet me so that I could be his guest at his comfortable lodgings. Since Reverend Humphrey R. Jones (whom I have mentioned before) lived nearby, I decided to send for him. He came immediately after receiving my message. Mr Jones is a tall, sturdy man and what hair is left on his head is completely white. He is not fifty yet, and although quite sprightly, he appears older than he actually is. He carried a homeopath medicine case which I presume contained about fifty small containers of powders and pills to treat all kinds of ailments. He brought this case with him to show it to Mr and Mrs Parry as he had bought it only the previous day in Oshkosh. He was hoping that this purchase could be used to bring much relief to suffering people.

'Mr Jones,' I said to him, 'It is a custom these days to gather information about Welsh people living in this country, that is, from the Welsh themselves. You have no objection to this request, I hope?'

Jones: Not at all.

Myself: There we are; you are an extraordinary character.
          Take your time to work out and note the main
          events, with dates from your birth to this day.

Jones: My parents were Hugh and Elizabeth Jones,
          Gwarcwm, near Trerddôl, Cardiganshire. They
          left their homeland and came to Oshkosh. I was
          born in Trerddôl in 1832 and became a church
          member there when I was ten. When I was fifteen,
          a religious conviction gripped me and I was
          persuaded to practise preaching the gospel, out of
          obedience to others, rather than of my own
          preference. The theme of my third sermon was
          based on I Peter, chapter 4, verse 18: 'And if the
          righteous scarcely be saved, where shall the
          ungodly and the sinner appear?' I was able to
          reassure seventeen people after this sermon. It is
          said that George Whitfield[2] converted fourteen
          with his first trial sermon. I preached in Ystumtuen
          and won over twelve; afterwards I preached in
          Mynydd Bach's chapel where several more
          became church members. I do believe that the
          Lord was guiding and blessing my ministry in
          north Cardiganshire at that time. I came to
          America in 1854. My family had already
          emigrated. Towards the end of 1856, I broke off
          my connection with the Methodist Conference[3]
          by following my own course in order to preach the
          gospel to all denominations, whenever
          opportunity arose. The place where I started in
          earnest as a revivalist was in Cambria, Wisconsin. I
          went there to attend a Wesleyan meeting and was
          persuaded by different denominations to preach in
          the neighbourhood's chapels. The first of these

services was conducted in Seion chapel (Congregational). All present, except one, stayed on after the service ended. A rumour circulated that I had stood in the doorway to stop people leaving. I would like it to be known that it was to the contrary. I actually announced that it was up to each individual whether they wanted to leave immediately or stay for a while.

I stayed in this region for about a month, preaching every night to ever more enthusiastic congregations. I moved on to Oshkosh, where Reverend John Parry (Congregational) accompanied and supported me for two weeks. I went from here to the Waukesha settlement and it was there the 'momentous dawn' broke. It was in Waukesha that my crusade had the greatest impact. I stayed there for six weeks before moving to the city of Milwaukee. I preached in Milwaukee every night and thrice on Sundays for one complete month. I was able to convince forty-five during this time. Afterwards, I spent one month in Racine and two weeks in nearby Pike Grove. I moved on to Big Rock, Illinois and spent three weeks there, preaching to Welsh and English congregations. During this time, I was invited to an annual service held by the Wesleyans in Oneida County, New York. I started a series of revivalist meetings there, starting with the Wesleyans and continuing with other denominations. On one occasion, Reverend Dr Everett (Congregational) told me that the spiritual climate had risen to an uncomfortable height; that the atmosphere was too overwhelming for children.

'How can I hold on?' Everett asked.

'Reassurance will come when the time is right,' I replied.

That night, it all happened. The unexpected effusions that grasped the congregation were so overwhelming that Everett and many others could not perceive what was happening or where they actually were. Six hundred and ninety souls were saved in Oneida at that time.

On my way back to my homeland, I was delayed for a month because I agreed to substitute for my fellow-countryman, John Ellis, who was ill at the time in New York. I did not hold revival services then, but thirty-five people of different denominations became church members under my ministry. After I arrived back in Wales, I preached thrice on Sundays and every weekday for a month in my place of birth. The Wesleyans gained ninety-five members and, in nearby Taliesin, forty-five joined the Calvinistic Methodists. I spent a month in Ystumtuen and Ponterwyd areas and almost 100 joined different churches in these villages. I came to Pontrhydygroes and Ysbyty Ystwyth where I met David Morgans. He was enamoured by the power of the spirit and became my assistant. One hundred and fifty returned to religion in those villages. In Mynydd Bach, forty-nine became church members. We went to Cnwch Coch and Cynon and I alternated my services between two chapels. Twenty-five returned to religion in Cnwch Coch and several more in Cynon. Afterwards, I stayed in Aberystwyth for six months conducting revival services; they were prayer meetings mostly. In Aberystwyth, approximately

600 people returned to religion amongst the Calvinistic Methodists; 150 to the Baptists; 120 to the Wesleyans – both English and Welsh; fifty to the Congregationalists and, according to Vicar Hughes, fifty to the Anglican Church. I was told that the vicar himself would have attended my meetings, if he had dared. Yes, 'If he had dared'. People in Wales know what is meant. Most people (not everyone, mind you) in Wales think that this division between Nonconformists and Anglican members is completely irrational.[4] In America, everyone, apart from Catholics, maybe, thinks it is beyond belief. After working so hard on the crusade, I became unwell and stayed in Aberystwyth for four years without preaching at all. Members of my family were concerned and told me to return to America, so that they could care for me.

I know that thousands of readers in Wales remember Mr Jones. I therefore feel justified in recording a section of this remarkable man's story in his own words.

---

[1] William Cowper (1731–1800: English poet and hymnodist.
[2] George Whitfield (1714–1770): Methodist evangelist.
[3] The Methodist Conference is the governing body of the Methodist Church.
[4] Nonconformists were those who did not conform – in other words, did not belong to the Church of England. They were referred to as dissenters or Nonconformists. By 1851, three-quarters of the Welsh population and a quarter of people in England were Nonconformists. Revivalism was a feature of Nonconformity in Wales. A powerful revival occurred in 1859 and an even more remarkable one in 1904–05. In the first half of the nineteenth century, a new chapel was opened in Wales every eight days.

15

Pine River; Blaendyffryn; the Mississippi; St Paul; Minneapolis

To go from Neenah to the Welsh settlement of Pine River, I had to board the train to Waupaca. It was obvious that I was in new territory. Social developments appeared everywhere – new clearings, new farms, new buildings and new villages. Nevertheless, the trees appeared old and their dark images on the lakes made the whole scene appear very sombre. I noticed that hedges and high fences had been erected. They had been constructed from tree stumps and roots that had been pulled out of the earth and intertwined in such a way that no hoofed animal could possibly cross over them. I remember seeing similar scenes in Ohio when I was a child.

Many Welsh people live in the Pine River area of 'Indian Land' as it is called by some. My compatriots seem quite happy with their lives but the land is rather barren and sandy and it is not possible to grow good crops here with the result that farmland is cheap. Those who seek low-priced, fertile land should go further west because rich soil, unlike unproductive earth, can be further developed and increased in value as population increases and conveniences are set up.

The Welsh in this region are very kind and supportive of the kingdom that is not of this world! The Methodist chapel, Salem, has a high membership; the building is spacious and has a decorative spire. A parsonage is being erected at present and Reverend Daniel Thomas, Radnor, Ohio, has been appointed minister and will take up residence in the new house. There is also a recently-built

Congregational chapel here under the ministry of Reverend Timothy Jones. The Baptist chapel in this neighbourhood has Reverend Robert Evans as minister. The Welsh who live here feel somewhat deprived of some of the advantages available to settlers in other parts of the country, for example, trading prospects and visits by religious ministers from Wales and other noteworthy travellers. However, reports are coming through that the railroad will soon reach the area; thereafter, religious and commercial opportunities should improve.

About 23 miles east of Pine River and 3 miles north of the town of Berlin, there is another Welsh settlement. There is better land here and two churches – one affiliated to the Congregationalists and another to the Baptists. The Welsh Methodist Cause has been discontinued in Berlin.

My next stop was Portage City, where there are a few Welsh people residing, but the Methodist Cause, like the one in Berlin, has been discontinued. The Honourable Llewelyn Breese lives in Portage City. He was Secretary of State for Wisconsin for two terms and has also filled other important positions. Another Welshman, the Honourable William Parry, has a large textile store here and is a member of the State Legislature. William Bebb, a native of Llanbrynmair, is another resident. These three men are elders in a Presbyterian church, although Mr Parry has not excluded himself from preaching in some of the Methodist pulpits.

Five miles south of Portage City, the Welsh settlement of Caledonia is situated – on the banks of the Baraboo River. The terrain surrounding this river is level and fertile, and overlooking the wide valley there is a beautiful plateau. A Methodist church has been erected here; Reverend Thomas Phillips, formerly of Pen-y-Cae, north-east Wales used to be its minister. Reverend Thomas Rice, a native of Borth, Cardiganshire, is in charge now.

Whilst travelling in the train from Portage City to Sparta, I noticed many interesting landmarks – large plains on both my left and my right; also perpendicular rocks rising to hundreds of feet above ground. These rocks vary in size; some are in clusters whilst others are sparsely positioned; others appear like lone owls that have been blinded by the sun! All their crowns are covered by greenery and wild flowers. It appears that in a bygone age this area was under water, since the stones resemble ocean rocks, and to this day shells are found on the sandy plains. Needless to say the land is not fertile and it is impractical as far as agriculture is concerned. The area is called Camp Douglas nowadays.

Eight miles south of Sparta, the Welsh settlement of Blaendyffryn is situated. This settlement is near the La Crosse River and is enveloped by rugged hills which resemble fortresses. The vegetation here comprises mostly of pine trees and other thin shrubs, amongst which a vast amount of wild strawberries grow. It appears that the soil in this area is ideal for cultivating strawberries. I believe that a keen gardener could make a very good living by growing soft fruits here. Once harvested, they could be transported very quickly by rail to the markets.

The terrain on the outskirts of Blaendyffryn has soil better suited for agricultural purposes and this is where you will find the Welsh farmers. A Welsh Methodist church has been established in the neighbourhood and contributing to the services, at one time, was the late Reverend Robert Williams. His daughter is married to Reverend H. P. Howell, Milwaukee.

Bangor is the next town on my itinerary where the Welsh reside. This urban district is full of freethinkers or German atheists while Welsh folk try to promote decency by keeping the flame alight on the altar. There are two Welsh churches in Bangor – one by the Calvinistic Methodists, under the ministerial guidance of Reverend H. M. Pugh, and a Congregational one, with Reverend John P. Evans ministering.

Three miles east of Bangor, Fish Creek is situated. People live here by tilling the land and they appear quite content. Mind you, it would be more profitable for them if they moved to a more fertile area. The Welsh Methodist chapel here is painted white and has a tall spire, which gives the building a dignified appearance. There are two other Welsh chapels in the area under the ministry of Bangor's clergy.

I have accomplished my appointments in the state of Wisconsin and I now look forward to the holiday I have arranged for myself. I am aiming at going west in order to assess situations there, so that upon my return to Wales I may be of assistance to prospective immigrants to this country. I must say that I was pleasantly surprised with what I saw in Wisconsin. It has more to offer than the eastern states that I visited. The south-east region has well-run farms and is a mixture of level plains, gentle hills, beautiful lakes and rich soil. The western expanse is more rocky and barren.

I set off on my new route by boarding the train to La Crosse, where I first set eyes on the Mississippi River. I was comforted along the way by the scenery and vegetation which made me imagine that I was back in Wales once more. After arriving in La Crosse, I boarded the train that ran along the west side of the Mississippi to St Paul, Minnesota – a distance of 130 miles northwards. It was impossible to see the other side of the river because there were so many islands covering the waters. Although these isles appeared paradisiacal with their greenery and tranquillity, it did not appear as if any people were living on them – only birds and wild animals. I had previously seen farmhouses on the islands of the Susquehanna River but there were no buildings visible on the Mississippi's islands at this point.

After travelling many miles, I noticed that there were fewer islands appearing and the entire breadth of the river was visible now. At one point, the river stretched like a lake and measured 5 miles from bank to bank with the length of the 'lake' being approximately 30 miles. Thereafter normal width of around a mile resumed. Below St Paul, the La Crosse River merges with the Mississippi which then becomes deeper and narrower, but if its width decreases, its beauty intensifies. Islands in different forms could be seen once more. Most of them were situated near banks as if they were trying to disguise themselves. Greenery covered their countenance, giving the impression that they were ashamed to be in the presence of such a majestic river. Other islands would appear bold – holding their heads up high like sugar-loaves commanding supremacy. It was a pleasure to see the steamboats sailing up and down the river and tied logwood floating downstream to the markets.

I shall not forget the first sight of St Paul as I viewed it from a distance. The Mississippi valley, at this point, stretches up to the hill upon which St Paul is situated. The scenery was amazing the morning I was travelling along, since there was a thin veil of mist down in the valley with St Paul's landmarks appearing above it. It would have been an ideal setting for any artist. St Paul is no different to any other city in the west. It is full of commerce, development and prosperity.

I saw several Red Indians in St Paul – squaws mostly. They had brought animal skins to the market to be sold or exchanged for white man's merchandise. I was tempted to speak to these ladies and I approached one that was crouching, since she appeared more Indian than the others. I asked her: 'Where do you live?' I must have frightened her because she picked herself up and ran to a nearby building with her face to the wall, similar to a small child who thinks that he is out of sight if he looks the other way. After not succeeding with that one, I turned to another two, who were leaning on a ladder, and I asked them the same question. They soon realised that I meant no harm because they smiled but did not say anything. 'No English?' I continued. They shook their heads and smiled again. As I walked away, I noticed that these two were having fits of laughter at the expense of the frightened one. They laughed and laughed until they were shaking and since one of them was quite plump, she caused quite a tremor – to put it mildly! The one that had been afraid realised that she had not been in danger after all, and soon returned to join the others with a peevish look on her face.

Ten miles up the Mississippi River, St Paul's twin city, Minneapolis, is situated. This is an amazing city with a population of 45,000 and constantly increasing. Many Welsh people have settled here and a Welsh Religious Cause has been established; a church building will be erected soon. The road between Minneapolis and St Paul is full of wonders and developments, with visitors arriving from all directions. One can swim and fish in clear lakes and there are splendid hotels, beautiful parks and promenades. Minnehaha Creek, a tributary of the Mississippi, flows west of Minneapolis. Minnehaha is an Indian name meaning 'the laughing stream' because of the way its waters prance about before reaching the renowned waterfalls called 'Minnehaha Waterfalls'.

16

Railroad Travel; Dakota; Mankato

After satisfying my curiosity with the wonders of St Paul and Minneapolis, I journeyed south-east for about 100 miles along the banks of the Mississippi to the town of Winona in order to join the Chicago and North Western line to Dakota. My mission was to explore new ground and I had expected that I would be in remote country by dawn but civilisation was evident, even at that early hour. Soon, we arrived in the town of St Peter. This town is at an early stage but its location on the banks of the enchanting Minnesota River is ideal in many ways. We travelled west from St Peter and I noticed that wheat was the main cereal-crop grown along the route. I expect the climate was too cold for maize cultivation. There has been a problem in Minnesota, the same as in some other states, with the chintz insect destroying crops.

If certain readers wish to make use of my Letters, it is advisable that they keep an eye on the map so that they can locate the places I am mentioning. St Peter is 435 miles west of Chicago; Sleepy Eye is 44 miles farther again, in the same direction. Although the area is sparsely populated, most of the land has been taken up and can only be bought as 'second-hand' from speculators or someone wishing to sell up and move on. Anyone purchasing land, in this area and at this time, should make sure that the title deeds are in order before any transaction takes place. Tracy is 46 miles west of Sleepy Eye. This stretch of land is quite exposed and not very fruitful, so it has not been populated to the same extent as some other areas. The government and the local railroad company are the landowners; terms and conditions regarding the purchase of land are varied and require much thought and understanding.

From Tracy, one branch of the railroad goes straight ahead to the west and another towards the north-west as far as Watertown, Dakota – 93 miles from Tracy. I continued my journey on the north-west line. The terrain surrounding this branch of railroad is hilly and very sparsely populated. Along the line, one finds villages every 10 to 15 miles. These communities are expanding at quite a pace; all have stores, mills, hotels, saloons, schools, chapels, and printing offices that are affiliated to different political parties. I was told that the inhabitants of these villages are old Americans. Whoever they are, they are far-sighted enough to realise that the adjoining countryside is being taken up rapidly and that commercial opportunities go hand-in-hand with a larger population.

Watertown, at the Chicago and North Western terminus, is only three years old, yet it is a big town with some large mansions. About 50 miles west of Watertown, one finds the fertile valley of the James River, and this is where settlers set their sights at present. The railroad will pass that way in the near future, but at the moment land is fairly cheap in this region and merchandise compares favourably with that found in stores further east. There are many beautiful lakes in the vicinity of Watertown.

To reach the other branch of the line in order to travel westward, I had to return from Watertown to Tracy; thereafter another 255 miles journey to Fort Pierre, which is situated on the Missouri River. The first part of this route, towards the town of Huron, takes one beyond the James River and through beautiful countryside. The neighbourhood of Lake Benton and the scenery between Minnesota and Dakota are most spectacular – clear lakes, beautiful bushes, open prairies, flat land and gentle hills which the Welsh would so appreciate, if only they had come over to occupy this region. Mind you, I must be careful as to the wisdom of my judgement. To have a full picture, I should be here at the end of August or during September when the crops are being harvested: 'Wherefore by their fruits, ye shall know them' (Matthew 7:20).

We travelled along through beautiful glades and found ourselves on open prairies. Before we reached Huron, we had to cross the James River; much is reported about this river's fruitful valley and many nationalities are directed towards this region to buy farmland. As far as the river itself is concerned, its bed, size and shape resemble any river in Wales. A branch of the Chicago and North Western line is being constructed at present and will run along the entire valley. I am sure this area will be highly populated very soon and land will increase in price as soon as the railroad is completed. However, I think immigrants should not be too rash when deciding which measure of land to purchase. They should weigh up all situations before making a final decision. No doubt, there will be many opportunities in this area once the railroad is in operation. If farmers in Wales, who are under oppression from wealthy landowners, as well as the ones in this country who have settled in less fertile areas further east, realised what possibilities this valley offers, a large Welsh settlement could be set up here. How can they be convinced, though? Maybe a plan can be organised – but I must move on to see other areas first.

Huron lies at the edge of the land which is being purchased and populated. We passed through the town's station and on to prairie land before we reached the Missouri River. There were small stations every 25 miles, until we came close to the river where the countryside forged into rugged hills, ravines, narrow valleys and fast streams that cascade between steep slopes. At last, we reached the eastern side of the river and were approaching Fort Pierre. Nothing spectacular can be said about the Missouri in this location; its width is just over a mile and, in my opinion, it resembles the Mississippi. What a place Fort Pierre is – the town's craftsmanship is excellent and every device has been implemented to make use of all available resources. Less than a year ago, it was just a small village; these days thousands of houses have been built on both sides of the Missouri. Apart from the stone and brick buildings, there are also wooden ones and some habitations are made from a combination of wood and turfs. Most of the homesteads have been well constructed, whilst some have been put together haphazardly with haulm[1] intertwined around their corner poles; the exteriors of these buildings are just boards put together and dabbed with mud or covered with turfs. Some shelters are built of turfs alone, whilst some people are still dwelling in canvas-covered wagons or just tents. Outbuildings are often used for all kinds of purposes such as saloon bars, billiard rooms and suchlike. The inhabitants of Fort Pierre come from all corners of the globe and are integrating into a neighbourly community. The reason many immigrants have chosen to settle in this region is on account of the railroad reaching out to the Black Hills where minerals have been excavated, and where productive meadows are plenteous.

As yet, the railroad has only reached Fort Pierre; one has to travel in what are called 'stages'[2] to reach places such as Deadwood, which is the most remote town in the Black Hills. I noticed that these stages – the carriage-stage which took us through the town and the barge-stage that ferried us across the river – had their exteriors blacked out in case of attacks by daring bandits. On the inner panels, there were narrow openings where passengers could peep without their faces being recognisable from outside. The journey from this spot to the Black Hills is not a very relaxing one since bandits often try to target a stage.

Goods are transported from this location to the Black Hills by six or seven wagons which are loaded and interlinked to form one long coach. As many as eight or nine pairs of horned oxen pull this coach and they advance *ling-di-long*[3], often egged on by the coach-driver's long leather whip if they start to flag. The poor creatures must be very sore and tired when they reach their destination.

Fort Pierre was flooded when the Missouri burst its banks last winter, yet the Americans are still building houses in the area. The attitude of these people can be compared to that of the builders of the Tower of Babel.[4] Fort Pierre is an ungodly place but its location, on the banks of the Missouri River and near the railroad to the Black Hills, is sure to increase its population and importance. I saw many Indians; they are the only people who dwell in this particular spot – on the west side of the river.

Whilst in Fort Pierre, I set my mind on going to southern Dakota. To accomplish this purpose, I had to go west for 400 miles to Mason City, Iowa, and thence 300 miles west again to Mitchell, Dakota. When travelling through Minnesota, my attention was drawn to what seemed to be straw or corn ricks in fields. Their size and shape resembled the ones I had seen in Wales. I was somewhat puzzled because the month was July, but after enquiring I discovered that these ricks were of last year's crop; winter had arrived early the previous year, before farmers had been able to thresh the grain harvest. Luckily, the ricks did not appear to be unduly damaged by the elements. Their crowns had been capped by snow, which had hardened and preserved them. Apparently, this situation has happened more than once.

My method of travel was with the Chicago, Milwaukee and

St Paul railroad. The line has been extended 50 miles further, and since no stations have been built as yet, this stretch has been named '48', because that is its mileage from Mitchell. This line will soon reach Chamberlain, a town on the banks of the Missouri, and thence to the Black Hills. The owners of this railroad are competing with the proprietors of the Chicago and North Western as to which one will reach the Black Hills first. These two railroads are amongst the most important ones in the world. They run parallel with each other and cross like a spider's web through the states of Illinois, Iowa, Wisconsin, Minnesota and Dakota. Although they are in opposition as far as business is concerned, they do co-operate and contribute towards populating the West and taming the wilderness. The state of Iowa has good prospects.

The amiable gentleman, Gwilym Eryri, Milwaukee, Wisconsin, has been promoted by the Chicago, Milwaukee and St Paul railroad to be in charge of the office that deals with immigration from the Old Countries. He is the one who advises the French, Germans, Scots, Irish, Welsh and English, and he does justice to all of these nationalities but is always very pleased to help the Welsh – his flesh and blood. It is gratifying to have a person who is one hundred per cent Welsh, without a trace of *Dic Siôn Dafydd*[5] in his nature, to be our guide in this business of settling in a new country. It was the lack of a good kinsman that caused the Welsh to be ushered to poorer regions previously, leaving the most productive lands to other nationalities. Another likeable and kind Welshman, John Meredith Davies, San Francisco, has been appointed Inspector General of the Chicago and North Western railroad. I understand that he is not directly linked to immigration but he can cross the line of duty to do favours to anyone who asks for help.

Mitchell is a new town situated about 3 miles west of the James River. Like Watertown, Huron and other western towns, it is progressing fast and, according to the rules and regulations that prevail, it aims at high moral standards. This can be said about most new towns that are situated towards the west of the country. The inhabitants are so busy building up their businesses in order to make a living that there appears to be little time for malpractices to enter their minds. Very fertile land is found in this region, but not many Welsh people have settled here. However, it is likely that there will be a strong Welsh community between Mitchell and '48' in the near future. Several immigrants from Wales have claimed land in this patch; one such person is Reverend John Moses, Waterville, Wisconsin. If anyone is interested in purchasing land in this neighbourhood, Mr Moses is only too happy to help and advise.

Because I had heard about the fertile land in Lyon County, in the north-west corner of Iowa, I decided to visit the region on my return from Mitchell. I left the train in Rock River Valley and since I did not know anyone in this part of the country, I decided to walk through parts of the prairies of Sioux and Lyon Counties. Ten years ago, I spent four months of solitude in the Canaan Rockies of Ohio Valley. I have also walked in the hills and on the seashores of Wales, mainly because of my love of nature's wildness. There is something very amiable in this kind of natural environment as it has been delivered by our Creator. This trek over the prairies, on my own, was right up my street. I made sure that I knew where I was, by keeping close to Rock River. I do not know why it is called thus as not many stones are visible in its waters or on its banks. There were plenty of wild fruits and weeds growing everywhere and that is always a sign of fertile land; I am sure that this region will be a good proposition for Welsh immigrants. This land is partly owned by the Chicago, Milwaukee and St Paul railroad company and partly by speculators. The price of land is between 5 and 10 dollars per acre and is well worth consideration at that price. Alongside the railroad, it is possible to buy cultivated land, together with farmhouses and buildings, at between 10 and 20 dollars per acre. Mind you, I would prefer to see settlers joining forces to buy land from the government, where opportunities and conveniences go hand in hand.

After walking many miles, I got tired of this hike and longed to put my head down, so I directed myself to Columbus City, Iowa – where, I believed, an aunt of mine lived (my father's sister). After arriving in Columbus, I discovered that my aunt and her family had moved to Red Oak five years previously. Therefore, I resumed my journey north-eastwards on the Chicago and North Western railroad through the states of Wisconsin and Michigan. After we passed through Green Bay, Wisconsin, all we could see was mile after mile of forestland. Some of the saplings were 12 feet high, full of leaves and the cheerfulness of summer, but as we travelled along, masses of old trees could be seen. Neither summer nor winter made any difference to them because they had lost their vibrancy, their bark looked like charcoal and their bare branches reached out in all directions.

After we passed the dead wood, the trees were of a different species. We could now see evergreens – cedars and pines. Much use is made of these trees since they boost the economy in this part of the country. Sawmills have been set up and the processed timber is shipped to Wales and other countries. Villages appear at random along the line and railroad stations have been set up. Apart from the charcoal kilns which are dotted here and there, the outdoor furniture and every other article were made of wood and there were stacks of timber in every station – all ready to be transported to different markets. Another important area of employment, in this district, is in the production of charcoal for use in the blast furnaces which are located near Lake Superior. The land is flat until the railroad is within 30 miles of the lake; thereafter rocky hills, rich in minerals, start appearing. I intend to pay a visit to another shore of Lake Superior at another time.

After a short break from duties I continued with my preaching commitments under the supervision of a small Methodist Assembly in Minnesota. The Welsh settlement here is called *Sefydliad y Coed Mawr* [the settlement of the great forest]. The Assembly covers more than Coed Mawr, though; the other section is in the beautiful Le Sueux district. The main source of income in both districts is tree felling. The residents living near the woods have to drain the waterlogged ground, whereas the residents of the prairie have to dig deep to draw water from the depths of the earth. Both communities seem quite happy with their environments and believe that their neighbourhoods will soon be lands of plenty.

Saron Chapel (Calvinistic Methodist) is in Coed Mawr and the parish has been named Sharon Township. The 'Rose of Sharon' and 'Lily of the Valley' flowers are in abundance in this area. On the prairie and 3½ miles west of Coed Mawr, Elim Chapel, another Calvinistic Methodist chapel, is situated. These two chapels are under the ministerial guidance of Reverend David Foulkes Jones, brother of Reverends Evan and Richard Foulkes Jones. The brothers are in Wales at present. Evan has returned to live in his native land while Richard is just visiting.

About 20 miles south-west of this region is situated the largest Welsh settlement in the state of Minnesota – Blue Earth. It stretches from Mankato in the east to Cambria in the west and is 20 miles long. The Welsh started settling here and in Le Sueur district about thirty years ago [around 1851].

They rented land from the government when they arrived, but now every acre has been purchased by the inhabitants.

The west part of the settlement is forested, but the rest is flat prairie apart from a few hillocks here and there. Our kin in this part are very happy with life in America, especially now that they are no longer plagued by locusts. At one time, the locusts were pandemic here. So far, the chintz insect, which has destroyed cereal crops in some parts of America, has stayed away from this area. It is not uncommon for gale-force winds and hailstones to be a problem at harvest time, though. These hurricanes cause much destruction as well as flatten crops, and are a danger to people and animals, since a hailstone can be as big as a hen's egg. In spite of some drawbacks, the inhabitants enjoy living here and do not believe in being too pessimistic.

The entire settlement is populated but commercial progress, on the whole, is rather slow. There is opportunity here for newcomers before land increases in price. Two Welsh churches have already been established. The price of intended farmland fluctuates between 5 and 25 dollars per acre, depending on condition, culture and the conveniences associated with the spot in question. The gales and hailstones are free!

I was in Mankato on 4th July this year, America's Independence Day. There was no joy in Mankato or any other town that day because President Garfield[6] had been shot two days earlier.

This town has a population exceeding 6,000 and a Welsh Calvinistic Methodist church has been established in its centre. Three miles south of Mankato lies the village of South Bend, where members of a small Congregational chapel and a Presbyterian church hold regular Welsh services. Situated in the neighbouring countryside one finds two other Welsh Methodist chapels – Seion and Carmel. I was invited to conduct a service in Carmel.

I did not expect to see large, ornate chapels in this rural area, so I was surprised to discover that Carmel was large and beautiful with a very decorative steeple. This chapel would not be out of place in a large city. Four miles west of Carmel is situated Jerusalem (Calvinistic Methodist). This is the main chapel in the settlement and it has a richly decorated interior. Reverend William Machno Jones is minister of this chapel as well as another, named Salem, which is situated 3 miles south of Jerusalem. The large village of Lake Crystal lies 3 miles south of Salem chapel and many Welsh people reside there, but there is no Welsh church in the village itself. There is a splendid Welsh chapel, by the Welsh Presbyterians, a mile west of Jerusalem, but I have been told that it is about to be closed down. Reverend Griffith Roberts is minister of Salem as well as the old chapel of Horeb, which is 2 miles north-west of Salem. I have been told that he is a very amusing preacher and I do believe that it was this man that Cranogwen[7] had in mind when she was speaking to me about a preacher who, in her opinion, was the best orator in America.

Cranogwen
(National Library of Wales)

Three miles west of Jerusalem Chapel is Bethel (Calvinistic Methodist). On 4th July many people sheltered from a thunder and lightning storm in this chapel. A corner of the building was struck by lightning. John D. Thomas,

Lake Crystal, was a casualty when lightning struck his shoulder, went down his side, his leg and through his foot before entering earth. Mr Thomas did survive but was bedridden for several weeks.

In Horeb's neighbourhood, *Siencyn Ddwywaith* [Jenkin twice] or Reverend Jenkin Jenkins, to give him his proper title, lives. He used to be a Congregationalist but has now joined the Calvinistic Methodists because there is no Congregational chapel near his home and he is elderly now. I have been told that the Methodists are very happy to have him as a member. Years ago, before it entered his mind to become a Methodist, he sympathised with the lack of funding which had befallen Horeb's members and he travelled hundreds of miles, without any reward, to collect money to pay off the chapel's debt. Some people condemned him because he was a Congregationalist supporting Calvinistic Methodists. His reply to that criticism was, 'It was not my fault that I was born in Mynydd Bach, Glamorganshire, and not in Llangeitho!'[8]

Reverend Thomas Foulkes, Wisconsin, was preaching in Horeb once and according to tradition in America, the collection in recognition of the visiting preacher was made at the end of the service. Horeb's minister asked Jenkin Jenkins to say a few words with the aim of persuading the congregation to give generously. Jenkins obliged, but did say that the minister would have been just as convincing if he had done that task himself. However, this is what Jenkins had to say:

The preacher has been sowing his earthly seeds at his home but he has come here to sow his spiritual seeds. The fact is, whilst he is away, various animals are eating his cereal crops and pigs are eating his potato harvest, so it is only proper that we all contribute handsomely.

On one occasion, Jenkin Jenkins was subpoenaed to be a witness for the prosecution at a court hearing. The case was of a man accused of felling his neighbour's trees. The lawyer who was cross-examining Jenkins was aggressive in his manner and tried to belittle Jenkins by insinuating that he was a greenhorn. The questioning went thus:

Lawyer	From what country are you?
Jenkins	That has nothing to do with this case.
Lawyer	Did you see this man cutting trees at the place in question?
Jenkins	Yes.
Lawyer	How many?
Jenkins	A few.
Lawyer	[agitated] A few, a few! How many are 'a few'? Can't you be more specific?
Jenkins	No.
Lawyer	Well, how many are 'a few'?
Jenkins	Less than many.
Lawyer	[so agitated) And how many are 'many'?
Jenkins	[mockingly] More than a few.
Lawyer	Who are you? Where did you come from? Where were you raised?
Jenkins	That is none of your business. Judge, please call this man to order?

The judge complied with witness Jenkins' request and the lawyer was reprimanded and became down-hearted for the remainder of the day. He was in no hurry to meet Jenkin Jenkins again!

Whilst I was approaching Horeb, I saw children and youngsters chatting outside the chapel. Two elderly men were also sitting on the steps. They were Jenkin Jenkins and another strange-looking man. Jenkins was slim and of medium height but the other man was short and stout with a large round face, a greying, patriarchal beard and piercing eyes directed at me. My matching stare did not affect him more than water on a duck's back. I came to the conclusion that this weird man was a genius or an utter fool. He was bare-footed, bare-legged and had other unusual attributes. Whilst studying his appearance and mannerisms, I came to the conclusion that he was a fool. I had never seen any adult, dressed like that, attending a church service before. However, to my great surprise, the person assigned to reveal the history of this region to the congregation, was no other than Huwco Hughes, the unconventional man. He must be a genius after all – a cousin of Dic Aberdaron,[9] maybe!

---

[1] Haulm: stems used for thatching roofs.

[2] The term 'stage' originally referred to the distance between stations on a route – the coach travelling the entire route 'in stages' – but through constant misuse it came to apply to the coach. As for 'carriage stages', a fresh set of horses would be harnessed every so many miles.

[3] *Ling-di-long*: slowly, often with a swaying movement.

[4] The builders of the Tower of Babel were in open defiance of God's command (Genesis, chapters 10 and 11). The tower was built about 106 years after Noah's flood.

[5] *Dic Siôn Dafydd*: a Welsh person who pretends that he has forgotten his native tongue and shows contempt for the traditions of his own race and country. The term is derived from a satirical ballad by John Jones (*Jac Glan-y-gors*) (1766–1821).

[6] President James Abram Garfield: twentieth President of the USA; shot in Washington DC on 2 July 1881 by Charles J. Guiteau; died 19 September 1881.

[7] *Cranogwen:* Sarah Jane Rees (1839-1916): schoolmistress, poet, editor, temperance advocate.

[8] A reference to Daniel Rowland (1711–1790): Welsh Calvinistic Revivalist. For most of his life he served as curate in the parishes of Nantcwnlle and Llangeitho, west Wales. His preaching caused turmoil and the Anglican Church officials threw him out. Following this, he established a Methodist Cause in Llangeitho. One of his great-grand-children was the novelist Anne Adalisa Puddicome (Allen Raine) (1836–1908).

[9] Dic Aberdaron: Richard Robert Jones (1780-1843). Polyglot; a native of Aberdaron. His father was a carpenter, but the son's apprenticeship to the craft was a failure. He became known for his exceptional knack of learning languages, ancient and modern, and also for his unkempt appearance and strange habits.

17

Minnesota; Perils and Pests; Farming; Lime Springs

It is appropriate that I mention an important piece of history that touched the Welsh settlement in Minnesota in 1862. The Indians were rebelling and murdering every white person that crossed their paths. No-one was spared and hundreds of men, women and children were killed. No doubt much blame rested on the shoulders of the government since the conflict [the Civil War, 1861–65] in the southern states made it difficult for it to fulfil its obligations to the Indians.

Since the majority of young men had enlisted in the Civil War at that particular time and the uprising by the natives was unexpected, the Indians were almost totally unopposed. The revolt affected only a fraction of Welsh people, but 10 September 1862 was an unforgettable day for them. A middle-aged family man, John Jones, was shot on the prairie as he was setting off to work, and the Indians excoriated his skull. Another elderly man was shot on grassland and his body was not recovered for several months; it was eventually found on one of the pyres the Indians had prepared. Another middle-aged man, James Edwards, on hearing the dogs barking, raised his brow to peep through a window and was shot straight through the head. Lewis Lewis, standing by a doorway in the same house, suffered a hand-wound as he tried to shield himself from the sun's rays. The son of Thomas Davies ventured to collect cows at milking time. His family were very concerned and watched him bringing the cattle down a hillside when they heard a gunshot and, at that instant, saw the boy fall to the ground. At one point, a few armed Welshmen and an Englishman, a Mr More, were confronted by Indians. An Indian fired first and More dropped dead. Other settlers suffered injuries and all these incidents occurred during one morning. Fear of the Indians had spread far and wide and people would congregate in strongly-built houses, venturing out only to feed and water their animals.

On 10 September, many Welsh settlers in North Minnesota left their homes and fled to South Bend Township, in the southern part of the state. They left their women and children, as well as the old and frail, in a mill and store premises before surrounding the buildings with boulders. The men encircled the site and prepared for battle with pitchforks, axes and any other suitable tool they could find to defend themselves from their enemy. Reverend Jenkin Jenkins lost five of his horses to the Indians that day.

Reverend Richard Davies (now of Mankato, Minnesota) was living farther south than most Welsh settlers in Minnesota. When he was travelling in a wagon through the woods one day, he realised the Indians were on his trail. He judged that he had enough time to disconnect the wheels off one side of his vehicle, hide them in rushes, and abandon the wagon. He then decided to take a different homeward route than was planned and he and his animals took off. When the Indians came across the discarded wagon, they decided to detach one wheel and fix it on the side that had been stripped. The result was useless, because that wheel did not match its opposite number.

Many people had moved away from the location where Reverend Davies lived and he persuaded his wife to do likewise. He stayed at home to look after the animals.

Once, when Davies was out walking and was some distance from his home, he caught sight of Indians lurking in grasses – waiting for him to pass by. Pretending that he had not seen them, he slowly made his way in another direction. He walked unhurried for quarter of a mile before realising that the Indians were following him. He immediately increased his pace hoping to reach the house of a Mr White. After he went over a hillock, he decided to lie in tall reeds that were growing nearby, hoping that his hunters would not see him. His plan was successful and he stayed in his hideout until it was pitch-dark. He then got up and started walking, without any idea where he would find himself. After a while, he came across a house where many robust men had gathered. These men were distrustful of him at first but after exchanging conversation, they realized that he was being hunted and in the same predicament as they were. After the men had listened to Davies' account of events, three of them decided to go over to Mr White's house to see if all was well there. Alas, they found the entire family dead, with blood all over the place; also valuable possessions had been snatched from the house. A group of men decided to hunt the guilty Indians, who had managed to escape – only by dropping their spoils on the way, though.

Between the grasshoppers, the whirlwinds, the hailstones and the Indians, our compatriots in this part of the country have experienced many upheavals. In spite of these disturbances, they have faith in this land. They are grateful that they are here and their hypothesis is that of Job: 'Shall we receive good at the hand of God, and shall we not receive evil?' (Job 2:10).

From Blue Earth, I went to the Welsh settlement of Lime Springs, Iowa – a part of it crosses over to Minnesota. The countryside in this region is a picturesque mixture of hills and plains and the Welsh started settling here about twenty years ago [around 1861]. They prospered for many years but the last four have not been profitable because chintz insects have been destroying crops. These insects are small, red creatures, slightly larger than fleas. They lurk in droves in the soil, around the roots of wheat, and suck sap and energy from the cereal grasses as they start to grow, thus stopping the grain from developing in the corn's ear. When wheat should be turning yellow at harvest time, one can recognise the crops that have been affected by chintz because white patches start appearing across the meadows; gradually complete fields turn pale. Although maize, barley and oats are not immune from this destructive insect, it appears that wheat is its main target.

Many Welsh settlers have failed in their agricultural enterprises because of damage to crops by chintz. The settlement on the Saratoga prairie is one example. When the Welsh arrived in this region, they bought as much land as they could afford by borrowing money. This was a good method if bumper crops could be guaranteed. However, spoiled crops resulted in low incomes and the annual mortgage payments were a struggle. Some borrowed more money, at a high interest – just to stay afloat. This method was often futile, resulting in repossession of land and well-built buildings. If an affected farmer owned animals and furniture, he would move to Dakota or another western region in order to obtain free land from the government. However, there is hope for farmers who have lost all assets and income. Employment prospects are good and high wages are paid to those who are healthy, willing to stay sober and work diligently. Doors are opening in all directions and expectations are high. Sometimes it takes more than one attempt to succeed, but this country has plenty to offer. This is the reason why Americans visiting Wales rejoice in their own achievements. I believe their ego is boosted by the fact that there are openings in America, rather than the actual amount of dollars in their pockets. As far as making a living is concerned, Americans know that they have enough elbow-room to pick and choose. Opportunities and independence lift people's self-importance wherever they live, whilst oppression and captivity make people undervalue themselves, creating a perception that circumstances are worse than they actually are.

A mistake the Welsh settlers have made in this region, as well as in other places, is purchasing more land than they can handle. Farmers have been securing as much as 320 acres without giving a thought to misfortunes that could come their way. These people have no financial cover when unexpected hardships cross their path. It is more sensible to acquire around 160 acres and keep some money aside for a rainy day. If a small farm shows profit at the end of a financial year, then purchasing more land is a wise move. I am sure that land in America will soon increase in value and the present very favourable purchasing terms will not be available in the near future.

Although the destruction of wheat by the chintz is the main hazard for farmers in this area, some crops have been affected by other destructive elements. Some believe that a difference in climatic conditions is a contributor. However, there are alternatives to these setbacks; good use can be made of land by rearing animals and growing flax, oats and maize. Wheat is the cereal crop most farmers are familiar with, and no doubt it is the most profitable when not blighted by insects or unpredictable weather conditions. Some farmers, who have had disappointments, do not wish to take chances by diversifying and have decided to move further west, with the result that land and farm buildings in Minnesota can be purchased at reasonable prices. There are opportunities here for anyone who wishes to rear animals rather than grow crops. The land is fertile, and amenities such as railroad, markets and other conveniences are at hand.

As far as Welsh religious services are concerned, they are well provided for. Two beautiful chapels have been erected in the settlement and both are well attended. These chapels are Foreston, at the centre of the community here in Iowa, where Reverends John D. Williams and Robert W. Hughes officiate, and Bristol Grove in Minnesota, where Reverend Owen R. Morris is in charge. In the village of Lime Springs, the Welsh worshippers assemble in the English Presbyterian Chapel. Reverend Richard Isaac is minister there. Churches with only a few members meet in vestries or school classrooms in some parts of the settlement. The Welsh would have erected more chapels if the chintz insect had not affected their incomes. All the Welsh churches in this settlement belong to Calvinistic Methodists.

I was staying in Reverend R. Isaac's home on 15 July when much destruction was caused by a ferocious storm which covered an area of 2 miles in width and 40 miles in length. I had never experienced such a combination of gales, rain, thunder and lightning. I could see saplings and maize compressed to the ground. The house shook and I had a feeling that I was on a 'free pass' to the lit-up sky! I was sure that the storm would be the topic of conversation at breakfast time the following morning – that is, if we were spared to see the break of dawn. Some members of the household thought that only the edge of the storm was hitting us. In fact, this was true.

We discovered afterwards that the eye of the storm was in New Ulm, Minnesota (population 3,500) – less than 100 miles from where I was staying. Most buildings and streets were reduced to rubble in New Ulm. As many as four houses were flattened in one sweep and blown away in a matter of seconds by the tornado. At least thirty-two people were killed and many more injured. Some suffered mental illness as a result of the fright and worry. Animals were knocked down and blown away by the whirlwind. I read in one of the Chicago newspapers that a live horse was found stuck up a tree. The climax came at five in the evening when the sky was filled with thunder and lightning and the town was thrown into darkness and chaos. Buildings, ricks, furniture, animals, poultry and all kinds of articles were crushed and hurled through the air. The noise was horrendous, with people screaming and animals bleating or neighing. The tornado sliced one girl's head off her shoulders as if a sword had caused the dreadful deed. Another girl was beheaded by a plank that was being tossed through the air by the gale-force wind. Bodies of men, who had been sheltering in houses, were found half a mile from their homes; even the foundations of the dwellings had been swept away.

Much devastation was also experienced in the countryside. Animals were killed and cereal crops, trees, buildings, ricks and farm implements were crushed and flattened. The tornado hit the west side of the Welsh Settlement of Blue Earth and several of our kinsfolk, in this spot, suffered huge losses on account of the tempest. The storm's duration at different points was between 15 and 30 minutes.[1]

I have stated previously that the Welsh in these parts

have been plagued by grasshoppers, hailstorms and all kinds of stormy weather, as well as attacks by Indians – in fact, more so than any other settlement in the country. It appears that the New Ulm district in Minnesota has been hit worst. Is it because of the Welsh people's association with the sinners of New Ulm? I wonder! It was Lot's friendship with Sodom's wrongdoers that caused his downfall.[2] Apparently, New Ulm and the surrounding areas are mostly inhabited by German Freethinkers. An entire township was created by them before any other white people settled in America. They vowed that no place of worship would ever be built in that region. However, after religious Germans settled there at a later date, they tried to build two chapels, but such was the opposition by the Freethinkers that the military had to stand guard before foundations could be laid. By all account, this neighbourhood was ungodly before the massacre by the Indians.[3]

Reader, did I not tell you when I started this mission that I had to double back and encircle a great deal as I travelled along. Well, from Lime Springs, Iowa, I journeyed almost 200 miles north to Minneapolis, Minnesota to conduct Sunday services. Do you remember the description I gave of St Paul when I first set eyes on it?[4] I was just as keen to witness the same picture this time round, but was disappointed. A difference in atmospheric conditions made such a difference to the view. A few days later, a gentleman in Brown County, Dakota, told me: 'If you were here on a clear day, you would see the town of Columbia appearing as if it was located in the sky!'

Since I have previously mentioned the beautiful city of Minneapolis, I shall now tell you of John H. Parry's account of events regarding his trip to Wales in the year 1873 – after living in America for twenty-five years. Mr Parry is a deacon with the Calvinistic Methodists in Minneapolis.

He posted a letter to his brother, Richard, informing him of his schedule. He wrote: 'I shall be leaving home on 5th June and sailing from New York on 7th. I shall be in Liverpool on 18th June.'

All arrangements went according to plan. After John Parry came off the train at Gaerwen, he heard a man telling the station master: 'I came here to meet my brother, who is visiting from America, but I doubt if he could possibly have arrived yet.'

'Who is that man over there?' the station master asked. 'He has grown foreign whiskers; maybe he is your brother.'

'Oh no, I do not believe that that man is my brother,' was Richard's reply. Nevertheless, Richard did approach the man 'with foreign whiskers' and asked him: 'Where have you come from, sir?'

'What!' the gentleman remarked. 'Are you as impudent as to ask everyone you see where he or she comes from?' Richard turned away and told the station master what this saucy stranger had said to him.

Richard Parry had his young daughter with him and she was all ears and eyes, anxiously waiting to see her uncle from America. She said to her father, 'That man is looking at us and smiling.'

'Well, maybe he is my brother after all,' Richard replied. 'John was always full of mischief.' Richard approached the man again and asked, 'Is your name John Parry?'

By now, John could not restrain himself and confessed, 'Yes, Richard, I am your brother.'

A few days after John's arrival in north Wales, he attended a concert, and when a certain gentleman was about to sing *Hiraeth Cymro Am Ei Wlad* [a Welshman's longing for his homeland], John Parry was asked to go up to the stage. As he did so, *Mynyddog*⁵ called out, 'Are you the man who tricked his brother?'

I wish to thank John Parry for that interesting tale.

---

¹ This storm occurred on 15 July 1881 and is similarly described by Reverend W. D. Evans in his book *Dros Gyfanfor a Chyfandir*, published in 1883. A translation of this book was published by Gwasg Carreg Gwalch in March 2008 entitled *Travels of a Welsh Preacher in the USA*.

² New Testament: II Peter (Chapter 2: 4-10).

³ 'Massacre' refers to the second attack on New Ulm by Sioux Warriors in 1870 when the inhabitants fled in a huge wagon-train to a fort thirty miles away. The Sioux burned New Ulm to the ground.

⁴ When Reverend W. D. Evans visited St Paul at an earlier time, there was a thin veil of mist along that part of the Mississippi Valley with St Paul's landmarks appearing above it.

⁵ *Mynyddog*: bardic name of Richard Davies (1833–1877): poet, singer and eisteddfod conductor.

18

Welsh Settlements in Dakota and Nebraska

Next in my diary is a train journey of 300 miles to Brown County, Dakota,[1] where many Welsh people have settled. Whilst travelling through southern Minnesota, I saw field upon field of ripe, undulating wheat – ready to be cut and tied into sheaves. The implements used were similar to those used in Wales except that they were bigger, heavier and more effective.

It appears to me that people in Wales are slow at learning how to tie sheaves, when in fact it should not be so. I was in Wales in 1872, when an exceptionally wet summer caused cereal crops to rot all over the country. I happened to be at my uncle's farm, Berthneuadd, Talsarn, on one of that summer's rare warm days, and I took stock of the workforce who had come to lend a hand with the harvest from the nearby villages of Talsarn, Dolbwbach and Llundain Fach. Each helper would make thick ropes from two lengths of straw. These lengths were placed alongside each other; then one end would be twisted, whilst the other end was held underarm. The ends were reversed several times before a rope was completed. Afterwards, the corn would be juggled about before it was made up into sheaves and tied with these ropes.

'For goodness sake,' I said. 'Why don't you find a quicker way to tie a sheaf? Since your crops are so essential and the harvest season so short, I really do think you should not waste so much time. I am sure I could manage to tie three sheaves for every one of yours.'

After I gave them a demonstration, the comment made to me was: 'Your sheaves are not as tight as ours.'

I was quick on the uptake, though and replied, 'Surely you do not want to preserve them until the end of time? My sheaves are sound enough to be loaded, to be made into ricks and will withstand throwing into the threshing machine. What more do you want?'

However, these folk would have the last word by telling me, 'Our sheaves are so sound that they can be thrown over houses and land intact on the other side!'

I decided not to pursue the argument further, since I was young and thought maybe there was some requirement to throw sheaves over houses at some stage, making them appear like crows flying through the air! Of course, I know better now. These remarks were said to pull the wool over my eyes since they must have regarded me as an inexperienced 'know-all'. To this day, I still do not understand why so much time has to be taken to tie sheaves in Wales.

I continued my travels along the banks of the Minnesota River on my journey through the west side of Minnesota. Soon afterwards, the train crossed over to Dakota and reached the beautiful, young town of Milbank. About 40 miles north-west of this town there is a large area of land which, up to now, has been an Indian Reservation. However, the Indians have come to an agreement with the government and have assented to 'move on', so this territory will be up for sale this coming autumn. These Indians have been allocated large areas of fertile land, but only for a limited period. As soon as native people are relocated, as is the custom, land is apportioned for use by pale-face folk.

To go west from Milbank, I had to board a freight-train because the passenger one does not go further than this town. This train took us over hilly, rocky ground with no plantations in sight and only a few houses could be spotted here and there. However, as we approached the James River, signs of civilisation increased. Two miles after crossing the river and we were in Bath, a town which is sure to be the market-place of the Welsh settlement. Bath is only a month old as yet, and most of it consists of housing made up of rough planks nailed together, whilst other shelters are merely canvas tents. The main store is located in a tent; nevertheless, a variety of good quality goods is provided by the shopkeeper. Another building, with the lower half made up of boards and upper half of canvas, is the hotel – a necessary place for visitors. I have also seen a long, low building which is the livery stable. Such a building is essential in this region, since land speculators require horses to take them over the prairies.

I discovered that the Welsh settlement was 4 miles north of Bath. I was there at dusk and the first house I visited was that of Robert Rowlands, the first Welshman to put down roots here. He arrived over a year ago and his family joined him several months later. Rowlands' house was considered lavish, and going by standards in force at the time, it was large enough to be divided into two rooms. The floor was covered with wooden planks and the interior walls constructed of boards which had been nailed together. The outer walls were 2½ feet thick and made of earth and turfs, in order to keep the house warm in winter.

Another Welsh settlement is being established in Lake County, Dakota. Most of Brown County's Welsh folk come from Cambria, Wisconsin; Lake County's Welsh come from Lime Springs, Iowa, and Davidson County's Welsh from the Waukesha area. The settlements in the east of the country are inhabited by an older generation of Welsh people, whilst the most recent Welsh settlers inhabit the most western states. There are exceptions to this pattern, of course. Many youngsters have followed their forefathers by sailing over from Wales recently.

To cross the Missouri River from Council Bluffs, Iowa, to Omaha, Nebraska, our train had to go over one of the most notable bridges of the Union Pacific railroad.[2] In 1854, there was only one log cabin where the vibrant city of Omaha is situated; nowadays [1881–82] it has a population of over 30,000. The city's first postmaster was a Welshman by the name of Jones. Apparently, he kept the mail in his hat. Nowadays, the Post Office is situated in a magnificent building. The city was named after the Omaha Indians who dwell in this part of the country. Omaha is an important commercial city with many railroads converging on it. William B. Hughes, from Bagillt, north-east Wales is a shop proprietor here. Very often a great many of the passengers are en route to California to seek work in the gold production business.

There are only a few Welsh people in Omaha – about thirty who are really fluent in the Welsh language and about the same who are *Dicsiondafyddion*.[3] There is a Welsh Sunday School here and an occasional sermon is preached in Welsh. Hopefully, Welsh religious activities will spread and increase in Omaha.

I commenced to the Welsh settlement of Blue Springs, Gage County, Dakota. Welsh people have set up home here over the past ten years and recently many came to this location to establish a Welsh community. It is the largest in the state of Dakota and is likely to develop further. There is beautiful countryside in this region with a mixture of plains and hillocks and although the whole area can be classed as a prairie, there are more streams and rivers flowing through it than I have seen anywhere else. The scenery is beautiful with evergreens growing on river banks. Maize is the area's main cereal crop although wheat and oats are also cultivated. As I travelled along, I saw a strange scene – cereal crops differing in condition from acre to acre. Some patches would be flourishing whilst others would not be thriving at all and at the point of withering. Some say that a difference in farming is one of the contributory factors for these variations, although some of the bad patches could be as a result of poor soil condition. I am glad to say that most of the maize was thriving; it is a good crop to grow in this country and very useful as animal fodder.

---

[1] Remember that Dakota had not been divided into north and south at this time.

[2] The first Union Pacific Bridge between Omaha and Council Bluffs opened during 1872, in some respects completing the Transcontinental Railroad.

[3] *Dicsiondafyddion*: Welsh-speakers who are ashamed of their native tongue.

19

Nebraska Welcomes Newcomers; Blue Springs

The new state of Nebraska[1] will be important to immigrants, since it is now welcoming newcomers. It lies at the centre of the United States and equidistant between Pacific and Atlantic oceans. The state enjoys a favourable climate on the whole, although I am told that snow did fall last winter. I was here in mid-summer when the temperature was above average. I felt quite comfortable myself and thought that weather conditions were comparable to those in Wales. The balmy breezes which blew over from the prairies made us all feel refreshed.

Since Blue Springs is the largest, most successful and most renowned Welsh settlement in Nebraska, let us hear what Welsh people living there have to say about the land. I approached Reverend James M. Pryse first:

Myself : What is your opinion of the condition of the soil in this state?

Pryse: Well, I think the top-soil is forced grass. Apparently, the surface was quite bare a few years ago. One notices gradual betterment as time goes by. Tufts of grass are appearing, and before long, grass will equal bare patches. Eventually, I am sure that grass and hay will be seen growing all over. When the ground is cut to a certain depth, a layer of black earth appears. Year after year, this black layer becomes thicker and thicker and can be dug up and used as manure for grassland and young saplings. It is true that trees are being planted by the residents these days, but trees grow of their own accord anyway. Look at the river-banks, there were hardly any bushes along them fifty years ago; today they shadow the water-ways and continue to expand. This is proof that this is virgin land and not one that has been depleted. This is excellent land.

I went on to approach Reverend Dr W. W. Jones:

Evans: How do you value the countryside?

Jones: My opinion is that land, like everything else, cannot be assessed by one glance. It has to be treated and nurtured before it is perfected. Sections of the subsoil, in this region, are rock-hard and this solidity is called 'hard pan'. Surface water is unable to seep through it and therefore all growth is hampered. The poor quality maize that you saw earlier had a hard pan underneath it. Man must improve the ground by draining it. There is also some alkali in this soil – a kind of poisonous salt that is detrimental to plants and animals. After this land is drained and the alkali flushed, I am sure that the whole countryside will flourish. Only certain parts of the subsoil are damaging, mind you. On average, there is no better ground to be had anywhere. Some people have dug up earth from the bottom of pits and wells, scattered it as top-soil and consequently produced excellent crops of hay, maize and other returns.

The next person I asked his viewpoint was farmer Owen Jones:

Owen: I go along with Dr Jones regarding the quality of soil dug up from certain depths. I dug a deep hole by my house one year and scattered the cleared earth as top-soil before sowing maize seeds in it. Needless to say, I had a wonderful crop. This proves that this earth is very fruitful. People are enjoying good health in this part of the country. One hardly ever hears of anyone suffering from fevers or diseases that often plague mankind. Nature only needs a little help at times.

This is how these residents praise their locality but this is the custom in every new community. People like to spread the word in order to encourage others to join them. This region has made an impression on me. We have not been troubled by stormy weather or grasshoppers. However, some careless people from Iowa have introduced the chintz insect to one patch. Let's hope the infestation does not spread. This part of the country suffers more from drought than dampness – a factor that is real to any region deprived of forests. I believe that plants and trees generate rainfall somehow. When a section of the Earth is populated, it calls on Heaven to quench its thirst, and when Earth is earnest, Heaven usually listens. Consequently, I believe that when more trees, hay, maize and other cereal crops are grown in Nebraska, the showers will fall and irrigate the land. Good land can be purchased here for approximately 10 to15 dollars per acre, and I strongly believe that immigrants can be persuaded to come this way. The villages of Blue Springs and Wymore are nearby, and two railroad branches going to the four points of the compass are within reach. Indeed, all necessary conveniences for running a business are at hand.

The inhabitants of this region are not deprived of religious services. A church, affiliated to the Welsh

Calvinistic Methodists, has been established and is on the up and up. The members erected a small chapel but it is proving too small and is being replaced by a larger one. Until recently, Reverend John Jones, a Cardi,[2] was the minister. At the moment, Reverend James M. Pryse, minister of the English Presbyterians in Blue Springs helps out; also Reverend Dr W. W. Jones and others, on occasions.

Reverend J. M. Pryse is very worthy of appreciation. He is one of the most able Welshmen in America, if not the world. Short and slight of build, he is approachable and kind but not too fussy about his attire and appearance. He is recognised by Americans as a very powerful debater and has taken part in fifteen important public discussions. He emerged as champion of each one of them. Even people who disagree with him admire his expertise. He respects people of all denominations who recognise and worship God but campaigns against atheism, deism, pantheism and suchlike. Catholics and Protestants have been protected from threats and challenges by him. He has an answer to every argument at the tip of his fingers and gets his opponents tongue-tied in no time at all. It is difficult to appoint anyone willing to participate with him in a public debate. I would not be surprised if a discussion between him and Bob Ingersoll[3] will take place soon, since I understand that Father Quinn, a prominent Catholic, would like Ingersoll to be challenged and has sent for Pryse in order to arrange such a meeting. A deliberation with Bradlaugh[4] would also be a spectacle. Reverend Pryse has suffered ill-health of late but I am glad to say that he is on the road to recovery. He is a powerful and amusing preacher.

Another minister, Reverend W. W. Jones, a Congregationalist who lives in Blue Springs, is a homoeopathist and hotelier. I have mentioned before that a hotel-keeper, in this country, does not necessarily mean someone who serves alcoholic drinks. Mr Jones' hotel is a temperance public-house. A piece of land bordering the Welsh settlement here belongs to Indians. This acreage will be on the market this autumn because the government has struck a deal with the natives, and as a result the present occupiers will move on. Many pale-face immigrants have set their sights on this terrain and it will be occupied once the government puts it up for sale. Hopefully, Welsh settlers will be able to secure it.

There are other small Welsh settlements in Nebraska, one in Aspinwall, Nemaha County; another in Salem, Richardson County; another called Gwalia Deg [fair dwelling place] in Clay County and another in Brush Creek. Welsh people occupy large sections of these places and there are Welsh religious services in some of them. Nebraska, like other American states, has Welsh people scattered all over.

To reach Red Cloud, about 100 miles west of Blue Springs, I had to go by bus in order to connect with a freight-train that shuttled along a stretch of railroad that had just been completed. As it happened, travelling on this railroad turned out to be a very bumpy ride. We were thrown in all directions and sometimes the train would stop and restart suddenly. The surrounding scenery changed so quickly that we did not know where we were. The effect of this weltering made some people laugh uncontrollably whilst others were not at all amused and appeared very sombre. Pictures of the train, depicting the manoeuvres it undertakes, appear on hoardings in several railroad stations.

Amongst us were two young mothers who had a baby each. When we stopped at a station, these young ladies thought they could relax and one had her baby on her lap whilst the other placed her infant across the seat. Suddenly, without any warning whatsoever, the train jerked resulting in both babies falling to the floor. When they were picked up by the frantic mothers, one baby had a nasal bleed and the other one's forehead had a graze. Their cries made everyone feel so sorry for the injured babies and their frightened mothers. Passengers were so angry that we were being transported in such a hasty, bumpy way – not that anyone took notice of such reaction.

Whilst we were travelling downwards at a gradient of 45 degrees, the train appeared like a gigantic horse plunging to a well to quench its thirst. Luckily, for all of us on board, the driver had reduced speed before two wheels came off their axles. As a result, we were stuck in the middle of nowhere for several hours while repair work was carried out. I made use of this unexpected free time by writing one of my Letters to *Y Faner*!

From Red Cloud, I went to Lincoln, the capital of Nebraska, and thence once more to Omaha. There was a very promising outlook on the land I journeyed through, with flourishing maize crops covering the fields. This region borders the state of Kansas and land can be bought for around 10 dollars per acre. Prospective buyers should be aware that not all of the terrain is fruitful; most topsoil appears in good condition but there are areas of poor subsoil in the state.

---

[1] Nebraska became America's thirty-seventh state on March 1st 1867. March 1st is St David's Day; St David is the Patron Saint of Wales.

[2] A Cardi: a person from Cardiganshire (as Ceredigion was called during the nineteenth century).

[3] Robert G. 'Bob' Ingersoll (1833–1899): Civil War veteran; American political leader and orator during the golden age of Free Thought; noted for his broad range of culture and his defence of agnosticism.

[4] Charles Bradlaugh (1833–1891): MP for Northampton, England, political activist and one of the most famous atheists of the nineteenth century.

20

Long Creek; Fflint Creek; Welsh Prairie; Williamsburg

I remarked about Iowa in a former letter when I described the surroundings of Lime Springs, Howard County. Apart from the ones mentioned before, Iowa has other Welsh settlements – one in Clay County, one in Green County and another prosperous one in Red Oak, Montgomery County. As yet, most of the Welsh settlements are in the south-east region of the state. This area differs from the north-western part since it consists of hills and crevices but it is possible to farm the area quite successfully. Wheat and oats are grown here for home consumption whilst maize and hay are the crops grown as fodder for animals, thus contributing to the sustainment of the holdings. Many Welsh farmers in this state have become quite affluent by rearing and selling livestock. Cattle and pigs are the main animals kept but those who breed sheep find that they are also profitable. The speckled red and white Durham[1] cattle are the ones mostly reared on the farms, but the hornless kind are becoming popular and it is considered that they will surpass the horned ones in the near future. Pigs kept in the western states differ from those in the eastern ones by their colouring. The ones in the west are usually black with white spots whereas the ones in the east are whitish: that is, when they have not been rolling in mud! I am made to understand that the white ones are hardier and less inclined to catch diseases such as cholera or some other deadly illnesses. In view of this, it appears that the white pig will be the popular one in the future.

Long Creek, the first Welsh settlement I visited in Louisa County, is one of the oldest in Iowa. The Welsh have been here for thirty-five years and they seem to be responsible and successful citizens. The settlement is about 6 miles wide and same in length and is situated in very pleasant countryside. Its waters are clear and a lovely atmosphere prevails. Columbus City, about 5 miles from its centre, is the market town and in nearby Columbus Junction, two railroads cross each other.

There are two Welsh churches in this settlement – Congregational and Calvinistic Methodist. The Congregationalists do not have a minister at present, but a retired minister and two preachers are members and they assist when services are held. The three of them are held in high esteem by people in the neighbourhood generally. Reverend Richard Hughes, son of the Honourable David Hughes, Yr Ynys, Carmarthenshire, is the Methodist minister. My opinion, and that of many others, is that Mr Hughes is dedicated to his work. He looks after his flock and is very approachable. I believe that his wisdom and cheerfulness do more good than a bucketful of medicine. Some people are so full of their own importance that they intimidate others, but Mr Hughes is like the sun, spreading light and warmth. An hour in his company is such a pleasure. It gives him so much joy to see others happy and he is at his best when spreading the Gospel. He is recognised as Father and Bishop by the new Methodist churches in the western states. He is also very supportive of Baptist and Congregational churches and considers their members as 'first rate' and 'first class'. These comments are reciprocated by all who know him.

Many miles south of Long Creek, there is a small Welsh settlement called Fflint Creek.[2] However, its culture and religion have anglicised so much that one can hardly call it a

Welsh settlement any longer. Around 60 miles north of Long Creek, there is a flourishing Welsh settlement called Old Man's Creek. Many successful Welsh people who settled about thirty-five years ago can relate to the hardships they encountered when they first put down roots here. One man told me that he actually lived here for a year without any money to his name and that he would not dare go to Iowa City without taking a sackful of maize-flour in exchange for something he needed. People had to strike a hard bargain for anything swapped for flour. All in all, it was an awkward situation, you may think, but no more so than the process carried out in my home country to this day. When I was over in Wales, I was astonished to find out how bargaining took place in fairs held up and down the country. There was a great deal of swearing and menacing behaviour taking place before any settlement was reached. After eventually coming to an agreement, another trickery was connived regarding the custom of 'luck' which entailed the vendor supplying the purchaser with a free drink, or if the purchaser was an abstainer, the 'luck' had to be given in cash and be of the same value as a drink in a tavern, otherwise the vendor would be considered as a very dishonourable man. It is a disgrace that reputable Christians have to succumb to such devious practices before they can sell something. I am voicing my opinion at Wales and not Ashkelon,[3] with the intention of throwing my hatling[4] towards the cause of persuading the dwellers of my native land away from these wicked customs.

Today, the inhabitants of Old Man's Creek enjoy many opportunities and privileges. Iowa City, its market centre, has more than 8,000 inhabitants with some of the Welsh residents being very responsible merchants. Two railroads cross each other at this location. The Congregationalists have erected a beautiful chapel here and although they are without a shepherd (apart from the Good Shepherd) at the moment, it is expected that a minister will be appointed in the near future.

About 20 miles west of Old Man's Creek, Welsh Prairie is situated. The Welsh started settling here about twenty years ago and it is said that there were hardly any inhabitants between it and Iowa City then – a distance of 20 miles. The valleys of the area were populated first of all. The settlement of Welsh Creek developed later because there is no river flowing through it. However, that disadvantage has been overcome since there are tributaries of the Iowa River in the region. By now, it is comfortably populated and has a small Methodist church with Reverend Thomas E. Hughes as minister. Several visiting preachers from Wales have held services in this church recently.

Ten miles further west is the flourishing settlement of Williamsburg. It was established about the same time as the settlements of Long Creek and Old Man's Creek. Agriculture is our compatriots' main industry in these areas. There is a prosperous Welsh Congregational church in Williamsburg under the guidance of Reverend J. Felindre Jones. Very notable clergymen have been ministers in this chapel – *Dewi Dinorwig*[5] being one. There is also a small Welsh Methodist church here and another in Welsh Prairie with Reverend Thomas E. Hughes acting as minister for both. He is held in high esteem by church members.

---

[1] The Durham breed of cattle in the nineteenth century, natives of the north-east of England, later evolved into the Shorthorn breed.

[2] Fflint is the Welsh spelling of the town and county of Flint in north Wales. No doubt people from this part of Wales had settled there.

[3] Ashkelon is one of the oldest cities in Israel. The place-name is probably Western Semitic, derived from the root 'ski' (to weigh) attesting to its importance as a centre for mercantile activities.

[4] Hatling: equivalent of half a farthing in monetary value.

[5] *Dewi Dinorwig*: Reverend Dewi Price (1804-1874), Congregationalist minister and author. He emigrated from Wales to the USA in 1857.

21

Des Moines; Beacon; Cleveland; Welsh Miners; Huntsville; Bevier; New Cambria

I continued my travels to Des Moines, capital of Iowa, and then 2 miles south to Sevastopol. In the latter, many Welshmen have occupations in the coalmining industry. There is a small Congregational chapel in Sevastopol and the services are held bilingually – half Welsh, half English. There are fewer Welsh people in Des Moines than there used to be. Apparently, most of the city's inhabitants are members of the Church of Jesus Christ of Latter Day Saints.

From Des Moines, I went to Oskaloosa territory. Many Welsh people have settled in this area. Most of them are occupied in the coalmining industry but some are busy earning their living by farming. Miners, on average, earn around two dollars (between eight and ten shillings) per day. Bituminous coal is the kind mined here, and for obvious reasons there is more demand during midwinter than at other times of the year although the miners are kept in employment throughout every season. There is a Welsh Congregational church in nearby Beacon, under the guidance of Reverend Isaac Hughes. He took up the ministry here recently and is settling down well. Gavin is another town south of Beacon, and the circumstances of the Welsh here are similar to those in other towns in the area. Reverend Hughes is also in charge of the chapel in Gavin and the services are held in Welsh and English in both churches.

Henceforth, I travelled to Ottumwa, where there are only a few Welsh inhabitants, and thereafter I undertook a long journey through rocky terrain to Cleveland, a small town in

Lucas County. This is another coalmining neighbourhood. The mines opened about four years ago and most of the miners are Welshmen. It is considered that this residential area will develop into a very important location. There is a Welsh Congregational chapel here but at the moment it does not have a minister.

There is also a Latter Day Saints church in Cleveland with a membership of around 100. Most of the members are Welsh although the services are conducted in English. Of the church's four elders, three are Welsh – the honourable John R. Evans being one of them. This church, which belongs to The Reorganized Saints, is very keen to demonstrate that it is quite different to the faith of the Latter Day Saints' movement founded by Brigham Young[1] in Utah. The church in Cleveland follows the doctrine of Joseph Smith,[2] which is an assertion that the 'New Jerusalem' should be situated on the banks of the Missouri and not towards the shores of Salt Lake, as Brigham Young proclaimed. I was given a copy of *The Book of Mormon* by the elder, J. R. Evans, and another friend gave me *The Book of the Doctrine and Covenants*. I found them interesting but was not conversant with the contents of either.

Readers of this Letter will find that the southern part of this particular region consists of fertile land and is therefore suitable for agricultural purposes. The ground is productive but has reached too high a price for newcomers. The given rate is from 25 to 45 dollars per acre these days. However, the farms provide ideal opportunities for young lads who want to gain experience in the industry. As yet, not many are interested and therefore good wages are paid to those who have engaged in the work. There is also employment in the coalmines, of course.

I should have mentioned that it was in the region of Old Man's Creek that the Welsh lectress, Margaret G. Roberts, dwells. She owns two holdings but does not farm herself now because she has enrolled to study at an Institute in order to prepare herself for public duties. 'The Entitlements of Women' was her initial subject, but now her interests are geology and astronomy.

The first place I visited in Missouri was Huntsville – a flourishing town, west of Moberly. As in many areas, coalmining is the industrial attraction for the Welsh and many have emigrated from Wales recently. Some are owners of coalmines whilst others are managers in the industry. Bituminous coal is the sort obtainable with the seam about 4 feet deep and approximately 3 miles wide; the seam's length is estimated at 70 miles.

There is a Welsh Methodist church in Huntsville; this Methodist church is the most southern place of worship that the Welsh have in Missouri. Mr Henry Williams, a student at The Presbyterian Park Institute, near Kansas City, is a regular preacher at this church.

From Huntsville, I travelled north to Bevier, a Welsh town on the Hannibal and St Joseph railroad and 6 miles west of Macon City. Again, coalmining is the source of income here. Thomas Francis, a native of Gwarcaeau, near Taibach, Glamorganshire, is manager of three mines in this area. The coal seam is a continuation of the one in Huntsville but the enterprise is more extensive here. A man, by the name of Hopkin Evans, was the first to embark in the coalmining business in this location and his dwelling is quite a spectacle.

There are many Welsh churches in this neighbourhood, and in Bevier the oldest belongs to the Congregationalists, with Reverend George M. Jones as minister. He is one of the area's pioneers and is well respected by everyone. The Welsh Presbyterians and Baptists are in the process of appointing two worthy men to take up positions as ministers in the near future. Reverend S. Pierce is working hard in the area and is focusing on Welsh and English speakers, coloured and white people – without any exception whatsoever.

Whilst several men had gathered together to tell me the history of the region, Thomas Francis asked me whether I was going to report all the information I was given, word for word. 'I shall aim at correctness,' was my answer.

Mr Francis replied, with a twinkle in his eye: 'We do not wish to report anything that is not respectable, therefore I ask you: is it proper for a Welsh minister to baptise Negroes?' I answered by making it clear to Mr Francis that ministers are instructed to act as propagate missionaries to every nationality dwelling on Earth, hence the question did not arise.

'If that is so,' Mr Francis continued, 'it is fitting that I tell you that many Negroes came to reside in this neighbourhood and since they did not have a minister to represent them, they approached Welsh ministers of religion to condescend to baptise them.'

'Condescend?' one Welsh minister proclaimed. 'I consider it a supreme honour to baptise any living creature, even if it was a mule, as long as it showed signs that it believed in Christ,' and without further ado, he officiated at a baptism.

Reverend Pierce asked me to quote the following verse which denotes the prejudice some Missouri people showed against coloured people:

Son am Pierce a glywir yma
Son am Pierce a glywir draw,
Pierce yn trochi dynion duon
Mewn dyfroedd llwydion ar bob llaw.

[Talk about Pierce is heard over here
Talk about Pierce is heard over there,
Pierce baptising black people
All around, in dark, murky waters.]

This poem was intended as harmless fun, yet it is time Christians considered every aspect of denominational prejudice with the same outlook as philanthropic people treat different groups of people. As far as religion is concerned, it is said that the Welsh have had a beneficial influence on some older, half-pagan American people of this region, since these people have aimed at adopting Welsh customs. The Sunday Schools of the Missouri people have elderly as well as young members and their inspectors advise them to look closely at the Welsh Sunday Schools in this country and to focus on emulating them. Many Welsh people fill important posts in this region, and there is a flourishing Mormon church in Bevier with many of its members consisting of Welsh settlers.

From this point, I went to New Cambria, the largest Welsh settlement in the state, situated about 10 miles west of Bevier. There are only a few Welsh people in the town of New Cambria itself, although there are two Welsh chapels there – Congregational and Presbyterian. The Baptists are in the process of erecting a chapel at present. Reverend G. Griffiths is pastor of the Congregationalists – a very able man, so I have been told. He was away in an assembly meeting when I was in the area, so I did not have the pleasure of meeting him. Many Welsh immigrants are expected in the Bevier area shortly and no doubt the Presbyterians and Baptists will appoint ministers in the near future.

Three miles in a southerly direction, there is a Presbyterian church called Salem, and 3 miles north there is a branch of this church, named Dyffryn [valley]. Seven miles north of Dyffryn, one finds the Glasston Presbyterian Chapel, named after the Welshman, John Glass, who had come over from Ohio. About 3 miles north-west of New Cambria, in Macon County, the Methodist church, Palmyra is situated. Moses Williams, one of the most stalwart pioneers of the region, is a member of this church. Mr Williams lived at one time in Palmyra, Ohio. Brushcreek's Methodist church is situated in the same neighbourhood and it is appropriate that it is called thus, because this area is almost entirely brushwood country. Brushcreek, Palmyra and Glasston churches are under the ministerial guidance of Reverend Edward Thomas. In order to be more financially viable, all Methodist churches in this area were united with the Presbyterians soon after they were established. At that time, they were situated some distance from other Methodist churches in the state of Missouri, but by today Palmyra and Brushcreek have reverted to Methodism once more. The Presbyterians are still holding on to their churches in Bevier, New Cambria and Glasston.

---

[1] Brigham Young (1801–1877).
[2] Joseph Smith (1805–1844).

22

Agriculture and Opportunity; Kansas City; Topeka

Agriculture is the main occupation in north-west Missouri. It is difficult to define the landscape, but on the whole it appears rough and unwelcoming and one wonders why the Welsh were encouraged to come to the region. A man by the name of Evan E. Roberts and his family were the first Welsh people to arrive and it took six years for anyone else from Wales to follow them. However, the supervisors of The Hannibal and St Joseph railroad were aware that one Welsh family had settled in the area and they were instructed to advertise land that was already on the market, in Welsh newspapers such as *Y Drych* and others. As a result of this publicity, many people emigrated from Wales and settled in this neighbourhood which they named New Cambria.

Evan Roberts asked me how I would describe the region. He approached me by saying: 'You can see it is hilly. Wales is also hilly but this area does not compare to Wales.'

'I shall say that Wales is hilly and New Cambria undulating,' was my reply. I continued: 'One can imagine the Welsh hills being positioned on flatland but this area appears as if the ground has been rippled.'

'Quite convincing,' was Mr Roberts' comment and he remarked that his impression of the area compared to a dozen snails placed higgledy-piggledy on a slate!

Many districts in this part of Missouri are unoccupied, with brushwood growing all over. Every year grass fires used to spread far and wide from prairie land, destroying all trees in their pathway. Prairie fires are not allowed to spread any more but strong roots are still in the ground and brushwood is growing from these roots. These uninhabited neighbourhoods are of good use to farmers because any number of animals can graze on them during summer months. During the autumn season, the animal owners have to make sure that crops have been harvested and stored to provide enough fodder for the winter months.

'Give me your honest opinion as to the wisdom of encouraging Welsh immigrants to settle on this land,' I asked Mr Roberts.

This was his answer:

I am not responsible for advising the Welsh to come to this area. The recommendation has come from the railroad's supervisors, although, I must admit that I did play a part on several occasions. The ground can be classified into three divisions – barren, moderate and fertile. One can notice soil in some districts appearing more flourishing than in this part of Missouri, yet in reality, it is often unproductive. The reason I have confidence in the ground here is due to the fact that it can hold and utilise manure. The earth consists of clay but it is moderate in texture – not too hard and not too sandy. An annual spread of manure works wonders on this subsoil, whereas manure added to some types of ground is often futile, in spite of the appearance of good topsoil.

All in all, I advise people to settle in this area because land can be purchased at around 20 dollars per acre.

A gentleman by the name of W. D. Roberts, who is General Superintendent of Livingston County, was the first to follow Evan E. Roberts and his family to this part of the country, and I asked his opinion regarding his assessment of the landscape.

He replied:

I believe that this region is as fertile as any area in America. Maize can be grown on lower ground and grass and hay on the slopes. There is no better place to rear animals. None of the Welsh has purchased barren land and I do not know anybody who has regretted coming here.

From this point, I went to Dawn, a village about 60 miles west. It is situated about 5 miles south of the town of Utica, which has the amenity of a railroad station. On the southeast side of the village there is a Welsh settlement. Land appears very fertile in this region with rolling countryside. One can see far and wide in all directions and everywhere that catches the eye is orderly and in good shape. This part of Missouri is well populated and land has risen in value from 20 to 30 dollars per acre. However, I did see some well-kept farms on the market for only 15 dollars per acre; the vendors were people who had been inhabitants for some time and wanted a quick sale because they had decided to retire or move away. Many enthusiastic Welsh farmers have worked hard and as a consequence are in a position to sell their land at reasonable prices. I must say that I am impressed by the appearance of the entire area.

There are six Welsh churches in this location – all within a radius of a mile. The Baptists are the strongest with Reverend R. M. Richardson acting as minister. The Congregationalists are close second with Reverend M. E. Davies ministering; the Methodists come third with Reverend Hugh Hughes in charge.

Seven miles from Dawn, the Welsh settlement of Low Gap is situated. The soil is also fertile in this locality but the railroad is not very accessible, which is a disadvantage.

There are Methodist and Congregational churches in the area and I had the opportunity of meeting Reverend Robert T. Evans, formerly of Nantglyn [a village in Denbighshire, north Wales]. He showed me a pocket-book he had received as a gift from Thomas Gee,[1] owner of *Y Faner* newspaper. He was very proud of his gift and took great care of it.

Drought is the main drawback in Missouri, as well as Kansas, Nebraska and other regions that are far from the ocean. Missouri does not experience much rainfall and drought does cause problems. This state was a captive one before the Civil War.[2] During the conflict, Welsh settlers had cause to fear for their lives and livelihoods. On occasion, enemy soldiers would invade their meadows but bushwhackers[3] were more of a threat than the soldiers. Even today, the people living in the most western parts of the state are harassed by these mobs.

On my way from Low Gap to Kansas City, my next destination, I had to travel through perilous countryside where gangs of thieves are known to pounce on stages and trains. Luckily, my journey was not interrupted. After arriving in Kansas City, in the state of Kansas, I became aware that I had turned up during the annual fair. These three-day fairs are held in every county throughout the country. Their purpose is to award prizes for best exhibits and performances in a variety of fields – animals, crops, fruit, machinery and so forth. The main attraction regarding this particular fair was a 15-mile horse-race between a Miss Williams and another young lady. Miss Williams had won a previous race, somewhere else, but it was the other Miss who was first past the post this time. She excelled in speed when swapping horses which was performed five or six times in all. I did not attend the fair myself but got to know all about it because no-one spoke of anything else.

Four miles south of Kansas City lies the village of

Rosedale where there are ironworks and furnaces. Many Welsh people live in this area but there are no Welsh services in local churches. Some worship alongside the Americans but I understand that the majority are 'having no hope and without God in the world' (Ephesians 2:12).

From Kansas City, I travelled over 60 miles west to Topeka, the capital of the state of Kansas. A State Fair was being held in this city, where the best item out of everything entered was awarded a prize. A horse race was also taking place. It was supposed to cover 20 miles but because one competitor was unwell, it was shortened to 10 miles. The race was between Miss Curtis, a Kansas lady, and Miss Pinneo from Colorado. Although Miss Pinneo was under the weather, she came in first but fainted afterwards.

There are many Welsh people residing in Topeka, and the ones who wish to worship their Creator join the Americans.

The date I decided to leave Topeka, I was delayed until the early hours of the following day because my luggage had not arrived from Kansas City. After everything was sorted out, I undertook a route which passed the village of Peterton and through a mining area where many Welsh people have settled, all belonging to different denominations: Congregational, Baptist and Methodist. They unite to hold services in one schoolroom. I eventually arrived in Osage City, just before dawn and after a little search, I found some compatriots. Although it was a Sunday, I must say there was only one thing on my mind and that was finding a bed, since I was very tired by now. I went straight to my room after finding suitable lodgings.

There are many Welsh people residing in Osage and Methodists and Congregationalists worship together in one chapel – one that they jointly own. They are ministered by two preachers from Arvonia, Reverend Davies (Congregational) and Reverend Evans (Methodist), who take it in turn to conduct services in this chapel. Most of the Welshmen who live in Osage are coalminers.

The day after I arrived in Osage, an acquaintance of mine, Hugh Davies, escorted me 12 miles farther to Arvonia, which is a small, scattered village surrounded by farmland. When it was reported that the Atchison, Topeka and Santa Fe railroad was to pass through the village, the community prospered and development took place. However, because the land where the station was to be placed was very expensive, the idea of bringing a railroad this way was abandoned and it was decided to take it through Reading, 6 miles farther. This change of plan resulted in land decreasing in value around Arvonia, with the consequence that people relocated in order to be nearer the railroad. There are signs that a rail-branch will be extended as far as Arvonia and the residents who stayed put are cautiously optimistic once more. There are some Welsh residents in Reading and a Welsh Religious Cause which is fluctuating between the languages of Welsh and English.

I was told beforehand that the land in this area was not as fruitful as had been expected. Maybe there is some truth in this observation but it does appear that many occupiers are happy with their world here. One sees large, prosperous farms all around and I have visited splendid homes where nothing is spared when the tables are laid. The ground is not a complete disaster either because some parts of the countryside are flourishing. I do not consider that all of the soil to be as fruitful as in some other parts of America because sections of it consist of a mixture of hard-pan[4] and gumbo.[5] When there is drought, wagons are taken some distance to a riverside and water is transported back to the residents and animals. Eventually, this problem will be overcome by sinking wells in the ground and assembling windmills to draw water up to the surface from these springs. All kinds of timber and firewood are scarce but coal is mined in the vicinity. The countryside can be described as 'rolling', and after the settlers have systematised the district with hedges, orchards, trees and so forth, the entire neighbourhood will have a very appealing appearance, I am sure.

In this part of the country, there are four Welsh churches in all, belonging to Congregationalists and Methodists. Reverend Evans, the Methodist minister, has been very kind to me. I also met Reverend M. B. Morris of Coal Creek, Colorado, during my stay here.

The famous minister and musician Tafalaw[6] resides in the Arvonia district. He attempted to address an audience once by lecturing about the history and philosophy of music but he failed to interest his listeners. His method of delivery was intellectual and monotonous but when he realised that his audience was finding his talk tedious, he said: 'What if I sing some amusing Welsh songs?'

His listeners woke up at once and feet were soon tapping and hands clapping when Tafalaw sang songs such as:

Mae gennyf geiliog bychan,
Mae gennyf geiliog mawr,
Mae gennyf geiliog arall
Heb fod yn fach na mawr.

    [I have a small cockerel,
    I also have a large one,
    I have another cockerel
    That is neither small nor large.]

The people, who had assembled to listen to Tafalaw, were now satisfied and went home in high spirits. If only I possessed the wisdom to Tafalaw sometimes!

Tafalaw

To go from Arvonia to Bala, I had to retreat as far as Burlingame, where I stayed overnight in a guest-house. The town was packed with visitors and I had to share a bedroom with a stranger. The following morning, the hotelier greeted me and said: 'I don't know if you realise it, but you slept in the same room as the County Sheriff last night.'

I replied that I had not actually *slept* in the same room as anyone, but if it was the Sheriff who snored in the other bed, tell him that I am lucky to be alive today, otherwise he would have a large quantity of mice to hang this morning; tell him also that he has an obligation to catch the fleas that feasted on my blood all night.

[1] Thomas Gee (1815-1898), Denbigh, north Wales: Calvinistic Methodist minister, journalist and politician.

[2] Missouri was a border state during the American Civil War (1861–1865) and saw the largest cavalry operation in American history; it was the scene of unparalleled guerrilla warfare.

[3] Bushwhacking was a form of guerrilla warfare common during the American Revolutionary War, American Civil War and other conflicts. It was particularly prevalent in rural areas.

[4] Hard-pan: a hard layer of earth, often beneath the superficial soil.

[5] Gumbo: a fine soil which becomes sticky or soapy when wet.

[6] *Tafalaw*: Thomas Gruffydd Jones (1832–1898): born at The Forge, Pen-y-cae, Monmouthshire. He was apprenticed as a carpenter but his chief delight lay in music. In 1850, he began to send his compositions to eisteddfodau and won prizes. He also became an eisteddfod adjudicator. After different achievements in Wales, he emigrated to the USA in 1866. In 1867 he was ordained minister of a Congregational church at Slatington, Pennsylvania and in 1869 he became Teacher of the Fine Arts at Emporia College. He served several churches in America before his death on 17 March 1898.

23

Bala; Emporia

After travelling 60 miles north, I arrived in Manhattan [Kansas]. To go to Bala I had to travel another 26 miles. Thomas Williams, the son of Thomas ap Gwilym, formerly of Pontrhydfendigaid, came to meet me, but because he thought I had travelled on another train, we failed to find one another, so I decided to start walking. The countryside reminded me of Wales. There were stone houses, stone hedges and rocks along the way. It was similar to walking along the shore in Merionethshire. In Riley Center, the night closed in on me, yet I had another 6 miles before reaching Bala. I plodded on under the moonlight and after covering a distance of 3 miles, I heard the sound of a wagon approaching. I was relieved because I thought maybe I would be directed by the driver or even be so lucky as to have a lift. The wagon did seem a long time before coming my way, but on a gentle descent, it suddenly accelerated and lo and behold, it quickly passed me by. I called out to the driver: 'Is this the road to Bala?' The driver and the boy who accompanied him ignored me completely, looked at each other and by making use of the whip, they galloped away. It was obvious that I had startled them.

After arriving in the village of Bala, I told people of my experience and described the two that I had seen in the wagon and their white horses. I had also noticed that they had tables on board. I was made to understand that I had probably seen Germans who lived nearby. However, a Welshman known locally as L.R. had another explanation. This man had told his wife that he had seen a man in a remote place and that he had urged his horses to speed up.

L.R. had been to Riley Center to sell pigs and he had cash in his pockets. The wife had been telling neighbours about the fright her husband had been subjected to and of his lucky escape! The following day, this account and my report of the incident, combined into one story – to the amusement of the residents of Bala, whilst L.R. was embarrassed and ashamed at the way he had reacted.

Bala is a Welsh village, thus named by the first settlers who had arrived from its namesake in north Wales. The surrounding agricultural land is called Powys. One side of the Welsh settlement is quite rocky whilst another part has hardly any stones visible on the surface. Many people are of the opinion that buying land in this district has not been a wise move. Many of the first settlers suffered because they bought land from a company called Cwmpeini Tirol Cymreig [Welsh land company]. Several honourable persons were members of the company but they had no prior knowledge of the business they had undertaken and their advice to immigrants was often just guesswork. This company bought land which they resold to the Welsh. It transpired that some of these transactions were not covered by authentic titles because of the administrative malpractices that had taken place; often people had to give up farmland which they had paid for in full. On the other hand, some immigrants have made good headway. Many people do indeed praise the area. The main handicaps, I believe, are the scarcity of water and firewood. Land fetches around 20 dollars per acre along riverbanks. The condition of the soil, conveniences and developments are always taken into consideration when holdings are up for sale. There is a Welsh Congregational church here under the ministry of Reverend Jones and also a Welsh Methodist church under the supervision of Reverend Morgan Williams.

From Bala, I travelled 80 miles south to Emporia, where

one finds the largest, most successful and most important Welsh settlement in the state of Kansas. There are around 6,000 inhabitants in the town of Emporia – many of them Welsh people who are admired by Americans. Many of our compatriots hold important positions as merchants and state officials. Mr L. W. Lewis, a bridge and railroad engineer lives here. He employs approximately 200 workers from Kansas City down to the state of New Mexico. He is originally from Aberystwyth and is an employer who makes sure he hires the Welsh when they arrive in the district he is engaged in. Although Mr Lewis is a successful entrepreneur, it appears that his priority lies in Religious Causes and the achievements of his compatriots. He is comparatively young and has a successful future ahead of him, I am sure.

There are two flourishing Welsh churches in Emporia. The Congregationalists have Reverend Henry Rees (formerly of Ystradgynlais) as minister and the Presbyterians are being cared for by Reverend John Jones (formerly of Rhydfach, north Wales). These two ministers have been in these churches since they were established and it does not appear that they wish to move on. There is good rapport between the two denominations: 'Behold, how good and how pleasant it is for brethren to dwell together in unity' (Psalm 133:1). The Welsh Presbyterians have one of the most adorned chapels in the country. This one is their second building as the first one was destroyed by fire soon after it was erected. Apparently, that one also was a fine piece of architecture. The Congregationalists' chapel is also beautiful.

Most of the Welsh farmers have settled in Cottonwood Valley, south of Emporia. They are succeeding in their venture. Their farms are orderly with well-kept buildings. I have been told that these farmers started up in business between 15 and 20 years ago with very little money. I used to know some of them when they lived near Newark, Ohio. They are now self-reliant and frequent the town to enjoy their profits. The lower land, which contains fertile earth, has been wholly occupied and if well cultivated can fetch around 40 dollars per acre. Some inhabitants who own animals, but do not possess any land at all, leave their animals to graze on open countryside that has no fences. There are four churches in the rural area; they are branches of the different denominations found in Emporia.

On Thursday evening, 29th September [1881] Emporia experienced torrential rainfall and everyone was so glad of it. However, about a mile northwards, a tornado erupted. A number of houses were demolished and five people were killed. I witnessed two bodies after they were brought to the town – a young bride, and a year-old child who had won first prize in a baby show a few days earlier. A similar tornado hit the other side of town three years previously when Reverend H. Rees saw a stable-building crash landing, after being hurled over an orchard without even touching a single tree.

From Emporia, I travelled about 100 miles farther to Burton, where there are a few Welsh people living – mostly farmers. It appears that the Welsh are doing well in this region. The terrain is completely flat here but parts of it consist of poor soil. Anyone unfamiliar with soil condition could be fooled to think it was of a better quality. The best way to learn about soil fitness is to consult Welsh people who already live in the district in question. Richard G. Jones and others can always recommend an area where the soil is rich. It is said that on the other side of the Arkansas River, 10 miles south of Burton, there is fertile land which can be bought quite cheaply and on easy terms. There is no Welsh church here yet, but my compatriots who have already settled in the area are anxious to establish one as soon as more people arrive from our native land. Like David: 'And David longed, and said Oh that one would give me of the water of the well of Bethlehem' (Samuel II. 23:15). Sometimes, a passer-by preaches a sermon in Welsh to my compatriots and immaterial of the sermon's content, they enjoy the offering as if an angel had presented it.

From Burton onwards, for mile upon mile, the terrain is a continuous plain, apart from a few hillocks towards the Arkansas River. Large sections of the earth and grass are white with alkali in the western part of Kansas and the soil is not as rich as that of the eastern region.

Kansas is a temperance state; its laws prohibit alcoholic drinks with the result that its towns are free from this beast. People, in their thousands, came to Topeka's fair from every corner of the state, yet there was no alcohol served. Mind you, I did see two lads who were quite tipsy. They had only just arrived from Wales, of all places, and had obviously gained access to illegal alcohol!

24

Colorado; Denver; Gwilymville; Leadville

The next step regarding Reverend W. D. Evans' peregrinations (recorded in Travels of a Welsh Preacher in the USA) *was his ascent and descent of Pike's Peak by foot, and his journey south on the Denver and Rio Grande railroad, on what was considered the most scenic line of America. He arrived in Monument, Colorado and went on to Gwilymville, a Welsh settlement, about 5 miles east of Monument's railroad station.*

He continues thus:

The Denver and Rio Grande railroad runs through the state of Colorado, which is the youngest of the United States of America. It was accepted in the year 1876, one hundred years after The Declaration of Independence.[1] It is therefore called the centennial state. The Rocky Mountains form a great part of it and the land surface is quite barren; nevertheless, it is full of natural minerals such as copper and tin of which the alloy bronze is made; also gold, silver, lead and coal. These minerals attract different kinds of skills and employment to the state. I shall now concentrate on my Colorado journey through Erie, Denver and Pueblo and on to Leadville.

Erie is a lively village in a beautiful glade. It is continually increasing as a result of lignite coalmining which takes place there. Miners are paid 3 dollars (12 shillings) per day, or 1 dollar 35 cents (5 shillings and 6 pence) per ton. This is the going rate for miners in most parts of Colorado.

There is an increasing number of Welsh people in Erie. They conduct religious services in the village hall and the members belong to different denominations. It is anticipated that a beautiful church building will be erected in this town in the near future. This Welsh congregation is being ministered by Reverend John T. Williams (Calvinistic Methodist), formerly of Coalport, Ohio and he renders his services for a low salary. Reverend Williams is a powerful preacher, nevertheless very unassuming. He has another occupation which is pharmacy.

Denver, the capital of Colorado, is situated about 30 miles south-east of Erie. It has a population of around 60,000 and is considered to be the most beautiful city of all the urban developments that lie between St Louis and San Francisco. It has attractive buildings, good roads and is situated on a lovely plateau – 5,000 feet above sea level. The main attractions are the Cathedral and the railroad's Union Depot and it is believed that there are only two better railroad stations in the entire country.

There are hundreds of Welsh people in Denver and there was a Welsh church in the locality at one time with Reverend J. T. Williams, Erie, delivering monthly services. The Welsh Cause has ceased by now but those who wish to serve their Creator, worship alongside the Americans who have zealous members in their churches. I understand that there is a desire to establish a Welsh society here to enable the Welsh settlers to come together. It was in Denver that the late Reverend R. L. Herbert spent the last years of his life. He was a literary man and well-known amongst the Welsh in America. He began his ministry with the Wesleyans but a difference of opinion caused a split between him and the Wesleyan hierarchy. As a consequence, he became a minister with the Unitarians and it is said that he was held in high esteem by his congregation and that church membership increased under his ministry. He was conscientious, serious, had high moral standards and his sermons were easy to follow. Much derogatory material was written about him by ministers of other denominations and some members of the public. He died last summer but his family still live in their grand home in Denver.

The settlement in Gwilymville was started by Gwilym R. Gwilym, from Glamorganshire. He discovered this location whilst walking through Colorado and New Mexico about eight years ago. Others joined him – relatives mostly – and by now there are ten Welsh families living here. The settlement is almost 8,000 feet above sea-level, therefore the altitude and climate are not suitable for growing maize, but wheat, oats and potatoes thrive in this location. Mr Gwilym has a dairy farm and has been awarded prizes in County and State Fairs for his cheeses. There is a feeling that the drought of the last two years has affected production in several aspects of farming. This particular area does have more rainfall than its surroundings because the pine and cedar forests attract rainfall and dampness. However, it is quite obvious that this region will have to be irrigated before more profitable crops can be grown and since there are wells and streams in the district this should not be a problem. I had the privilege of conducting a service in the Gwilym household. Mrs Gwilym is from this area and is the daughter of the late John Cartwright of Denbigh, north Wales.

So far, it appears that the Welsh who have settled in Gwilymville are doing well. They live in comfortable homes but it is not likely that other farmers will see fit to join them since the settlement is small and I am sure that there is better land elsewhere. These Welsh settlers are actually isolated, living in a lovely, quiet valley, without any communication with the outside world. It does not appear that they are bothered about religion either but they do comment that they would welcome a preacher, if one came their way. Most of them are Methodists but they do not consider denomination a problem so long as the cleric himself is honourable. They have commented that someone like the late Reverend R. L. Herbert would suit them. A good example of religious liberalism indeed, since Reverend Herbert was a Unitarian minister in his latter years. Another example of this kind of generosity was the fact that some time ago, the Welsh Trinity Church in this state actually split into two equal divisions with the hope of appointing a new minister to the recently-erected chapel. The outcome resulted in the chairman of a certain committee using his casting vote in favour of Reverend Herbert, rather than a well-known Trinity minister. What would the people of Wales say about a decision like that! I, myself, am not passing any judgement whatsoever; I am merely recording what happened as news because these events will go down in history.

From Gwilymville, I travelled to Monument Park, the Cave of the Winds, Cheyenne Canyon, Williams Canyon and Glen Eyrie before arriving in Pueblo. It is said that many Welsh people live in this town. The Hughes brothers are renowned timber merchants and Daniel Jones is a reputable manager in an iron mill. As yet, there is no Welsh Religious Cause here but it is hoped that there will be one shortly.

Until recently, I was travelling southwards but by now my romantic railroad journey took me north-west towards Leadville and Gunnison. I stopped in Coal Creek which is 35 miles from Pueblo. There are hundreds of Welsh people in this town. Coalmining is their main occupation and the miners earn good money. The two coalmines in the area are owned by the railroads Atchison, Topeka and Santa Fe, and Denver and Rio Grande.

The coalmining manager of Atchison, Topeka and Santa Fe is Colonel Sauvage, a Welshman, whilst the under-manager is another compatriot by the name of William

Thomas. The villages of Rockvale and Oak Creek border with Coal Creek. Many Welsh people live in these three communities. A flourishing Welsh church was established here four years ago. The minister is Reverend Morris B. Morris, son of Evan Morris, Wern – of the Foel district, near Cann Office [a village near Llangadfan], Montgomeryshire, and a brother of Reverend John Morris, Ebbw Vale, Monmouthshire. When Reverend Morris started his ministerial work in this area about three years ago, church membership was dwindling but as a result of the minister's influence and God's grace, attendances soon increased and as a result the church is doing well. The services are held in Welsh and English in a beautiful building which was paid for by faithful members. I stayed with Reverend Morris and his family for almost two weeks.

I continued with my journey through the Royal Gorge and when darkness fell, I stayed in Salida,[2] and on my return, in Buena Vista. I wanted to make sure that I was in both places during daylight. I thence continued to The Twin Lakes, which are situated below Mount Elbert,[3] and onwards to Leadville, an urban area which has developed as if overnight. Seven years ago, the spot was just uncultivated land. Now, a city has been built and the population is over 40,000. Gold and silver are mined in the surrounding mountains.

Hundreds of Welsh people live in Leadville and a small Welsh church saw to their spiritual needs at one time. Alas, this church has ceased to function and very few of our compatriots pay heed to righteousness, temperance and justice. They prefer to join the evil practices that prevail in this ungodly city. This fact applies to many people scattered across Colorado and other western territories. People have arrived from Wales and from the eastern states with Church Transfer Letters in their pockets and devotion to God in their hearts. However, after arriving in these parts, other concerns occupy their minds. Their intention of becoming church members goes by the way and sooner or later the pubs and other dissipations have more appeal to them than churches and chapels. This has become the pattern with the Welsh in many parts of Western America, I am afraid. It is becoming a way of life, to a certain extent, in places like Coal-creek, Erie, Russell Gulch and other areas where Welsh religious services do take place to this day. Indeed, the Sabbath is the most profitable day of the week for the local pubs. Much talk and writing takes place in Wales about the Foreign Mission and about sending missionaries to India, China and Madagascar, and sympathy is expressed towards people of these distant lands, but what about our own people? Don't you know, back in Wales, that in Denver, Leadville and other places in America, many of our compatriots are in a worse state than the pagans of India, as far as conduct and morality are concerned? Surely, missionaries of the same blood and language should set their sights at America rather than focus on countries whose languages are foreign.

Having reported the negative aspect of the customs of my fellow-folk in this country, I must not forget that there are some honourable Welsh people in Leadville as well as other towns and cities in America. James H. Morgan, a native of Glamorganshire and a very sincere gentleman, lives in the state of Colorado. He has given me several specimens of minerals and stones. Also, in Colorado, Thomas G. Roberts, son of Reverend Griffith Roberts, Minnesota is a much respected merchant and Charles Pugh is a responsible supervisor in one of the mines.

There are no Welsh settlements as such in Colorado, but many Welsh people live in places like Central City, Russell Gulch (where there are two Welsh churches), Black Hawk,

Idaho Springs, Alpine, Georgetown, Kokomo, Golden Silver Cliff, Gunnison and other places. Underground workers from some American states like to try their luck by relocating these days. They land in certain places like a cluster of black birds but rarely stay put for long. At present, most miners set their goal towards Colorado and other western states and I wish them well. I am sure that materialistically they will benefit, but they should not be tempted by evil trends which can influence some folk.

---

[1] The Declaration of Independence was adopted by the Continental Congress on 4 July 1776. It stated that the thirteen American colonies, then at war with Great Britain, regarded themselves as independent states, and no longer part of the British Empire.

[2] Salida is in Chaffee County, Colorado. The Arkansas river flows through this county carving its way into the granite canyons of Chaffee. It is the fourth longest river in the USA.

[3] Mount Elbert is the highest peak in the Rocky Mountains of North America at 14,440 feet.

The End of the Story; Obituaries

Reverend William Davies Evans' mission was nearing its end and he made his way back through various states to New York. He boarded the City *of Berlin in New York harbour and sailed back to Liverpool, England. He went thence by train to Aberystwyth where he was met by his family. After he settled back in Wales, he delivered lectures on his discoveries and experiences in America.*

In Baner ac Amserau Cymru *(2 June 1886) a reporter writes thus about a lecture entitled 'The Wonders of the Far West', which W. D. Evans delivered in Pontmorlais Chapel, Merthyr Tudful, at the end of May 1886:*

> 'The Wonders of the Far West' was the title of a lecture which was admirably presented by Reverend W. D. Evans at Pontmorlais Chapel, last Tuesday evening. I, myself, was unable to be present but I have heard such good reports about the talk.

William Davies Evans died in December 1907, in Tacoma. His activities from 1886 onwards are described in the following obituary. This is a combination of two obituaries that appeared in Y Drych *(by Reverend J. Michael Hughes), and in* Y Cyfaill. *The obituaries were written 'so that people in Wales and across America would know of Reverend Evans' passing and his eternal faith in his Creator'.*

**Obituary of Reverend William Davies Evans
who died at his home in Tacoma, Washington,
on 16 December 1907**

On Monday, December 16, at his home, 1911 North Anderson Street, Tacoma, Washington, after suffering a long illness, Reverend W. D. Evans died. He was born in Wernfach, Talsarn, Cardiganshire on February 23rd, 1842. In 1852, when he was ten years old, he went over to America with his parents. In 1867 he started preaching in Columbus, Ohio, and the following year he enrolled at Delaware University College, Ohio. In 1870 he continued his studies at the Institute of Theology in Oberlin, and was a regular preacher in the district of 'Jackson and Gallia', Ohio. During this time he was also put in charge of churches in Youngstown, Weathersfield and Churchill.

In 1872 Mr Evans returned to Wales, making his home in Llanilar, Cardiganshire. On 13th August 1874, he, as well as twelve other young men, was ordained at a Methodist Assembly Meeting which was held at Rhydfendigaid's Methodist Chapel, Pontrhydfendigaid. Taking part in this service were Reverends Owen Thomas DD, Edward Matthews, William Williams, Swansea, and Howell Powell, New York. He married Jane Jones, Penwernhir, Pontrhydfendigaid, in 1876.

Towards the end of 1880 Mr Evans returned to America but sailed back to Wales again in 1882, after making his way across the breadth of the United States. During his stay in America he was guest preacher in Welsh churches in many states. Collecting material for the book *Dros Gyfanfor a Chyfandir*, which he later published in Wales, was his main mission during this period.

After settling back in Wales once more, he remained in his homeland for five years and was inducted as the first minister of Llanfihangel-y-Creuddyn's Cynon Chapel. He also preached as a guest preacher in other chapels across West Wales.

In 1887 Mr Evans returned to America – with his family,

Cynon Chapel

this time. In 1888 he embarked on establishing the paper *Columbia* and was editor of this paper for almost four years. After this accomplishment he regularly officiated in services throughout the county of Jackson, Ohio. In 1894 he took charge of churches in Long Creek, Iowa, and from 1895 to 1899 he was minister of churches in Williamsburg and Welsh Prairie, Iowa. From 1899 until 1903 he took charge of churches in Elim and Sharon, Minnesota, before setting up home in Tacoma, Washington. Sons Alfred, Hugh and David made sure that there was a comfortable home for their parents in this city. During 1904 and 1905 he preached and took care of the Cause in Carroll.

This report is a brief account of Reverend W. D. Evans' activities and occupations in Wales and America. Apart from his work as a minister of religion, he was also a literary man. Every article he wrote proves that he maintained his own independent views about different issues. His last printed sermon in *Y Cyfaill* was interesting and related to present-day affairs. Respecting his wishes, Mr Evans' funeral was modest with no flowers. He did not want anyone to write a biography of him.

Acknowledgements

I wish to thank friends and family in Great Britain and the United States of America for their support during the time I have spent selecting, translating and compiling the 'Letters' my great-uncle, Reverend W. D. Evans, despatched to *Baner Ac Amserau Cymru* in the nineteenth century, in order to publish this translation of his work.

My special thanks go to Ivor Wilks, Nancy Lawler, Huw Walters, Nicola Taylor, David Lloyd, W. Arvon Roberts, Paula Monsef, Judi Dunham, Gwen Day, Jill Tomos, Hugh Matthews, Christine Trevett, Aled Davies, John Pritchard, Lyn Ebenezer; helpful staff at The National Library of Wales, Aberystwyth; Myrddin ap Dafydd and all the staff at Gwasg Carreg Gwalch, especially Jen Llywelyn.

Further books of interest

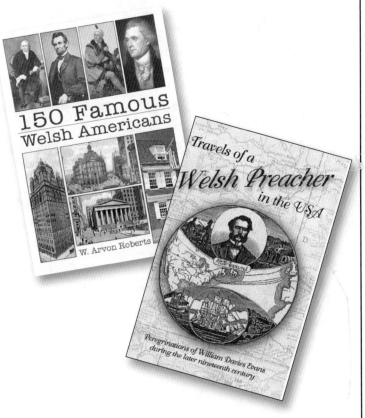

Visit our website for further information:
www.carreg-gwalch.com

Orders can be placed on our
On-line Shop